WHERE PITTSBURGH PLAYED

OAKLAND'S HISTORIC SPORTS VENUES

DAVID FINOLI, TOM ROONEY,
ROBERT EDWARD HEALY III, DOUGLAS CAVANAUGH
AND CHRIS FLETCHER

THE
History
PRESS

Published by The History Press
Charleston, SC
www.historypress.com

Front cover, top left: courtesy of the University of Pittsburgh Athletics; *top right*: courtesy of the Pittsburgh Pirates; *middle*: courtesy of the Pittsburgh Pirates; *bottom*: courtesy of the University of Pittsburgh Athletics.
Back cover, top left: courtesy of the University of Pittsburgh Athletics; *top right*: courtesy of Duquesne University Athletics; *bottom*: courtesy of the Pennsylvania Trolley Museum.

First published 2022

Manufactured in the United States

ISBN 9781467151467

Library of Congress Control Number: 2022936638

Notice: The information in this book is true and complete to the best of our knowledge. It is offered without guarantee on the part of the authors or The History Press. The authors and The History Press disclaim all liability in connection with the use of this book.

CONTENTS

Acknowledgements   7
Introduction   9

I. FORBES FIELD (1909–1970)
1. Pittsburgh's Grand Stadium: Oakland's Forbes Field
   May Have Been One of the Most Important Stadiums Ever Built,
   by Chris Fletcher   15
2. An Annual Love Affair with Forbes Field, by David Finoli   22
3. Phil Coyne: Baseball's Only Hall-of-Fame Usher,
   by Dan Coyne   25
4. In the Shadow of Maz's Home Run, by David Finoli   28
5. A Season of Ineptitude: The 1967 Pittsburgh Phantoms,
   by David Finoli   31
6. Face's Last Stand, by David Finoli   34
7. For the Heavyweight Championship of the World:
   Ezzard Charles versus Joe Walcott,
   by Douglas Cavanaugh   37
8. Rooney-McGinley Boxing Club: Bringing Fights to Oakland,
   by Douglas Cavanaugh   39
9. Stop the Ballgame: Fans Listen to the Billy Conn–Joe Louis Fight
   at Forbes Field Before the Pirate Game,
   by David Finoli   42
10. Josh Gibson: The Greatest of All Forbes Field Hitters,
    by Thomas Kern   45

11. A Pandemic Contest to Remember: Pitt Crushes Defending
    National Champion Georgia Tech, by David Finoli   48
12. Of Steagles and Carpitts: The Steelers Make Their Way
    through World War II at Forbes Field, by David Finoli   51
13. Don't Take Anyone for Granted: Carnegie Tech Stuns
    Knute Rockne and His Irish of Notre Dame,
    by David Finoli   53

II. PITT STADIUM (1925–1999)
14. In the Shadow of the Cathedral of Learning:
    The History of Pitt Stadium, by David Finoli   57
15. Better than the Best?: Duquesne Upsets Eventual
    National Champion Panthers at Pitt Stadium,
    by Robert Healy III   62
16. The Day the On-Campus, Off-Campus Debate Began:
    The Pitt Stadium Finale, by David Finoli   65
17. There Used to Be a Basketball Arena Here: The Pitt Pavilion
    Is Built Underneath Pitt Stadium, by David Finoli   68
18. The Fruitless Venture Finally Ends: Pitt Scores against Fordham,
    by David Finoli   71
19. A Picture for the Ages: A Bloodied Y.A. Tittle Kneels on the Turf
    at Pitt Stadium, by David Finoli   74
20. Pie in the Sky: Pitt's Tony Dorsett Helps Bring the Program
    from the Basement to a National Championship
    by Slicing Up an Old Rival, by Chris Fletcher   77
21. Steelers Say Sayonara to Oakland After 1969 Season,
    by Tom Rooney   80
22. We're No. 1: Pitt Beats Army and Ascends to No. 1 in the Polls,
    by David Finoli   83
23. The Track John Woodruff Called Home, by David Finoli   86
24. Revenge Is Sweet: The Pitt-USC Rivalry in the Sutherland Era,
    by David Finoli   89
25. The Greatest Coach Ever to Roam the Sidelines at Pitt Stadium:
    Jock Sutherland, by David Finoli   92
26. On the Heels of a National Tragedy: The 1963 Pitt–Penn State
    Matchup, by David Finoli   96

III. THE FITZGERALD FIELD HOUSE (1951–PRESENT)

27. Replacing the Ice Box: The History of the Fitzgerald Field House,
    by David Finoli   101
28. Building a Championship Program at the Fitzgerald Field House:
    Pitt Volleyball, by David Finoli   105
29. The Peery Dynasty and the 1957 NCAA Wrestling Championships,
    by David Finoli   109
30. "Send It in Jerome": Jerome Lane's Famous Backboard-Breaking
    Moment, by David Finoli   111
31. The Forging of a President: Two Key Campaign Stops in Oakland
    Fuel the Legend of JFK, by Chris Fletcher   113
32. When the City Game Was Great: Pitt-Duquesne Basketball at
    the Field House, by Robert Healy III   116
33. Playing Like National Champions: Pitt Cruises Past the
    Soon-to-Be National Champion Villanova Wildcats,
    by David Finoli   119
34. A Big East Baptism: Pitt Upsets St. Johns, by David Finoli   121
35. What a Coach Should Be: Pitt Wrestling Coach Rande Stottlemyer,
    by David Finoli   123
36. Country's No. 2 Team Falls to Duquesne at Pitt Field House,
    by Robert Healy III   127
37. Going Out in Style: Duquesne Perfect in Last Two Years at Home
    at Pitt Field House, by Robert Healy III   130
38. The Greatest Game That Didn't Count: Duquesne Basketball
    Defeats the Pittsburgh Pirates…Wait…Huh???,
    by David Finoli   133
39. Making a Statement: Pitt and WVU Play Their Last Backyard Brawl
    at the Fitzgerald Field House, by David Finoli   137

IV. THE DUQUESNE GARDENS (1890–1956)

40. The Duquesne Gardens Was Fertile Ground for Sports of All Sorts:
    The History of the Duquesne Gardens, by Tom Rooney   141
41. The NBA Comes to Pittsburgh…and Then Disappears,
    by David Finoli   146
42. A Busy Day in the 'Burgh: The Pirates Open Forbes Field,
    Then Fans Walk the Short Distance to the Duquesne Gardens
    to See Heavyweight Champion Jack Johnson Take on Tony Ross,
    by Douglas Cavanaugh and David Finoli   149

43. A Pittsburgh Fight Extravaganza: The Conn-Zivic Fight,
     by Douglas Cavanaugh   152
44. Sugar and Spice: The Great Sugar Ray Robinson Takes on
     Sammy Angott, by Douglas Cavanaugh   154
45. Sonja Henie Comes to Pittsburgh: The Ice Capades Are Born
     at the Gardens, by David Finoli   156
46. A Black and Gold Lovefest: The Yellow Jackets Morph into
     the Pirates, by David Finoli   159
47. Chick Davies or Dudey Moore: Who Was the Greatest
     Basketball Coach at the Duquesne Gardens?,
     by David Finoli   162
48. The City of Champions: 1955 at the Duquesne Gardens,
     by David Finoli   165
49. All Signs Point to the End: The 1956 AHL All-Star Game,
     by David Finoli   168
50. Indoor Tennis Begins in Pittsburgh Earlier than You Think:
     The Fred Perry and Ellsworth Vines Show Comes to
     the Gardens, by David Finoli   171
51. The Best Play Here: Duquesne Gardens Hosts Dukes Cagers
     as Nation's No. 1 Team, by Robert Healy III   174
52. "TV Basketball Parties Everywhere": Live Cameras Capture
     Dukes Topping Bonnies in Battle of Unbeatens,
     by Robert Healy III   178

Appendix A. It's Miller Time: In the Pre-Internet Age,
     a New Season Meant a Trip to Gus Miller's Newsstand,
     by Chris Fletcher   181
Appendix B. First or Not: Greenlee Field Housed Champions,
     by David Finoli   185
Bibliography   189
About the Authors   191

ACKNOWLEDGEMENTS

Creating a book is certainly an effort that brings the passion of the subject out in the people who tell the story. This one was no different for the five authors who tell the story of these four great facilities in the Oakland section of Pittsburgh. As much effort as it took us to put this book together, its completion could not have been done without the help of others.

With the time we put in over and above our normal workdays, a thank-you goes out to our families and friends for the support they gave us throughout the process. This couldn't have been achieved without them.

There was Duquesne University's David Saba, E.J. Borghetti of the University of Pittsburgh and Jim Trdinich of the Pittsburgh Pirates, who generously allowed us to use the photos in the book. Their photo donations are very much appreciated.

We also would like to thank Gary Bolin, Pat Santoro, Rob Ruck and Joe Gordon, as well as authors Dan Coyne and Thomas Kern, who did an outstanding job writing the stories of Phil Coyne and Josh Gibson in the Forbes Field section of the book. We also want to thank the many others who helped us with the various chapters of this book.

Finally, we'd like to thank The History Press, especially our acquisitions editor, Banks Smither, and editor Rick Delaney, who have been incredible partners for all of the books me and the group have written for this outstanding publisher. This is the twelfth. Without the help of all, this book would not have been a possibility.

—David Finoli

Babe Adams was in his rookie year when Forbes Field opened in 1909 and finished with a 12-3 mark. Despite his good season, he wasn't expected to start in the World Series. But he became the star of the Fall Classic, starting and winning three contests as the Bucs captured their first title. *Courtesy of the Pittsburgh Pirates.*

INTRODUCTION

Walking past the Forbes Field wall behind Posvar Hall on the campus of the University of Pittsburgh while preparing for our book on the Civic Arena, *Pittsburgh's Civic Arena: Stories from the Igloo*, it hit me just how close the major sports facilities in Oakland were to one another for the first half of the twentieth century.

I really wasn't sure where the Duquesne Gardens had been situated. I wanted to do a chapter on it as the Arena's predecessor, so I looked up the parameters and began to walk from Forbes just to see the proximity. I found it across the street from St. Paul's Cathedral and was amazed it was as close as it was. To make my venture complete, I walked up to the site where Pitt Stadium stood and then over to the Fitzgerald Field House, which opened in 1951.

As a sports fan, I thought this would have been fantastic—having everything so close, every sporting event you could possibly want to see only a few blocks away. As excited as I was, I began to concentrate on the Civic Arena book and put my thoughts on Oakland sports facilities on the back burner. That is, until I got a phone call a couple of months later.

That was the day Tom Rooney gave me a call and began to discuss the potential for a book about the sports facilities in Oakland during that time. It was fate telling me that a book had to be done on these historic places.

Developing a table of contents for the proposal was exciting—so was pulling together a phenomenal group of writers who would make this an incredible anthology. We were lucky enough to have Douglas Cavanaugh,

After years of coming up short in the national championship quest, the Duquesne Dukes finally won their first in 1955. They defeated their rivals, the University of Dayton Flyers, 70–58, in the finals. *Courtesy of Duquesne University Athletics.*

one of the country's elite boxing historians. He suggested a chapter on the day Forbes Field opened, which was also the evening that heavyweight champion Jack Johnson fought at the Duquesne Gardens. It was a day that really told the story of how exceptional it was to have all the facilities so close together. Robert Healy III took most of the Duquesne University chapters to celebrate our alma mater. They both joined Tom, myself and former editor and publisher of *Pittsburgh Magazine* Chris Fletcher to form an outstanding team.

Once our friends at The History Press took a look at our group of writers, the proposed table of contents and the proposal and agreed that this was a great idea for a book, the project was born. The book would tell the story, in essence, of the history of sports in the Steel City between 1909 and 1961 and would, appropriately, be titled *Where Pittsburgh Played: Oakland's Historic Sports Venues*, as Oakland was truly its epicenter.

Many of my favorite projects are those in which we learn more about stories that we had known only on the surface. And this one fits that bill. We had the joy of researching subjects like the radio broadcast of the Conn-Louis fight at Forbes Field and the little-known game at the Fitzgerald Field House that might have been the most exciting contest played at the facility. It was an exhibition contest pitting Duquesne University and Fort Belvoir. The latter had three college basketball greats, Dick Groat, Johnny and Eddie O'Brien, all of whom played for the Pittsburgh Pirates in the 1950s. Other great stories include the indoor tennis match between two of the game's stars at the time, Fred Perry and Ellsworth Vines, that sold out the Duquesne Gardens in 1937; a celebration of the Peery family at the 1957 NCAA Wrestling Championships; and the life of one of the greatest and most admired coaches in Pittsburgh history, Rande Stottlemyer.

With those stories and so many more, we proudly present to you our new project!

—David Finoli

I

FORBES FIELD
(1909–1970)

Catcher Smoky Burgess dives into the stands to catch a ball in game six of the 1960 World Series while the Yankees' Mickey Mantle (no. 7) looks on. Burgess was selected to play in the All-Star Game during the season and hit .294 for the world champions. *Courtesy of the Pittsburgh Pirates.*

1

PITTSBURGH'S GRAND STADIUM

Oakland's Forbes Field May Have Been One of the Most Important Stadiums Ever Built

By Chris Fletcher

Barney Dreyfuss had a problem. Specifically, the owner of the Pittsburgh Pirates in the early 1900s had a stadium problem. His team's Exposition Park, located close to where PNC Park now stands, was a disaster waiting to happen. For one thing, it flooded constantly. It wasn't unusual for outfielders to be ankle-deep in water. The facility was constructed of wood, so fire was a constant worry. And Exposition Park just didn't hold enough fans. Even in the dead-ball era, owners wanted to do everything they could to maximize profits.

So, on March 1, 1909, after securing a tract of land originally part of Schenley Park, crews broke ground on what would become Forbes Field. Just four months later, the team hosted the Chicago Cubs before a record crowd of 30,388.

Forbes Field (Dreyfuss resisted naming it after himself, instead choosing a hero from the French and Indian War) ushered in the era of modern ballparks. To celebrate that achievement, here are sixteen fun facts about Forbes Field.

DREYFUSS MADE "IF YOU BUILD IT, THEY WILL COME" COOL WAY BEFORE *FIELD OF DREAMS*

Choosing to build his new stadium in Oakland instead of close to downtown Pittsburgh was a huge risk. Oakland was nine miles away, a considerable distance in 1909 with its limited modes of transportation. But Dreyfuss rightly reasoned that the city would grow to meet him. With universities, green spaces and museums, he bet that Oakland would be a desirable place to be. Forbes Field soon became a centerpiece of the area.

IT WAS A TECHNOLOGICAL AND ARCHITECTURAL MARVEL

Forbes Field revolutionized stadiums. It was the first stadium made completely of concrete and steel.

A three-tiered grandstand extended from behind home plate down both the first- and third-base lines. It was one of the first ballparks to have luxury suites, located on the third tier of the grandstand. It was the first to have ramps to take people to their seats and elevators to take patrons to the third level.

One level of seating extended to both the left- and right-field foul poles, and bleachers were located in left and center fields. It was massive. The original dimensions at Forbes Field were 360 feet (left), 462 feet (center) and 376 feet (right). The red-tinted slate roof in right towered 86 feet above the field. The park, with its buff-colored terra-cotta and light-green steel façade, was wedged into its Oakland neighborhood.

IT HAD ITS SHARE OF QUIRKS

Unlike the next generation of cookie-cutter stadiums, Forbes Field had its share of charming and not-so-charming features. After batting practice, the batting cage was rolled out to center field, some 420-plus feet away. The 14-foot Longines clock with speaker horns on top of the left-field scoreboard was out of play. Any drive that hit it was a home run. The scoreboard was manually operated. The metal numbers that fit inside it are treasured collectibles.

The infield was rock hard. Announcer Bob Prince referred to it as "alabaster plaster." A bad hop off the infield hit Yankees shortstop Tony Kubek in the throat and was a turning point in the 1960 World Series.

IT STARTED THE SUCCESSFUL STRING OF NEW PITTSBURGH FACILITIES

The Pirates capped Forbes Field's inaugural season with postseason success. Led by Hall-of-Fame shortstop Honus Wagner and the pitching of rookie Babe Adams, who tallied three victories, the Bucs won their first World Series in seven games over the Detroit Tigers.

Forbes Field started a trend. Three Rivers Stadium and Heinz Field both hosted playoff series in their opening seasons, though both the Pirates (1970) and the Steelers (2001) didn't advance to the World Series and Super Bowl, respectively. As for PNC Park, well, never mind.

IT WAS THE HOME OF THE FLYING DUTCHMAN FOR FIVE DECADES

Although Wagner retired following the 1917 season, he was a permanent fixture at Forbes Field. At least his locker was. His locker and uniform remained there through the 1952 season.

IT WAS THE SITE OF THE FIRST PROFESSIONAL BASEBALL BROADCAST

On August 5, 1921, Westinghouse engineer Harold Arlin called the Pirates' 8–5 win over the Philadelphia Phillies. Pioneering radio station KDKA carried the broadcast, with Arlin set up with a microphone in the stands. It began a one-hundred-year love affair between baseball and radio.

IT HOSTED NEGRO LEAGUES GAMES, FIGHTS AND OTHER EVENTS

Sure, Forbes Field is best known for being the home of the Pirates. Also calling the stadium home were: Pitt football (1909–24), which won five national championships while playing there; the Homestead Grays of the Negro Leagues (1922–39), capturing four titles; the Steelers (1933–42 and 1945–63), including when the team combined with the Eagles (1943) and Cardinals (1944); the Pittsburgh Americans of the now-defunct AFL (1936–37); and the Pittsburgh Phantoms of the NASL (1967).

Forbes Field also hosted a number of fights during Pittsburgh's golden era of boxing. Hometown boy Fritzie Zivic faced off against Jake "Raging Bull" LaMotta. Another local fighter, Billy Conn, successfully defended his heavyweight title against Melio Bettina. From 1910 to the mid-'50s, the stadium was a boxing hot spot. One of the biggest matches was the 1951 heavyweight championship, in which Jersey Joe Walcott beat Ezzard Charles in seven rounds to win the title.

For a Pitcher-Friendly Ballpark, There Were No No-Hitters and Only One Cy Young Award Winner

It's a bit of an anomaly. Forbes Field, with its gargantuan dimensions—particularly in the power alleys—was considered a pitcher's park. But throughout the years it spawned its share of rakers, including Wagner, Pie Traynor, Paul and Lloyd Waner, Ralph Kiner and Roberto Clemente.

There was never a no-hitter in the stadium. And only Vernon Law won a Cy Young Award, for his 1960 campaign, when he posted a 20-9 record for the world champs.

It's Where Babe Ruth Hit the Final Three Homers of His Storied Career

On May 25, 1935, a broken-down Babe Ruth had his last hurrah, and it happened at Forbes Field. Ruth, exiled from the New York Yankees and now part of the Boston Braves, clubbed three home runs, including a bomb that was the first to clear the stadium's right-field roof. The ball traveled an estimated six hundred feet (although that could be a legend). Oakland resident Wiggy DeOrio claimed to have picked up the ball blocks away from the park. He later donated it to the National Baseball Hall of Fame in Cooperstown.

Bing Crosby Sang There Almost Every Night during the Summer

Crooner Bing Crosby eventually bought a stake in the team. In the 1950s, a recording of Crosby singing the national anthem was a regular pregame feature.

THE TEAM ADJUSTED THE FENCES TO HELP RALPH KINER AND HANK GREENBERG, BUT FORBES FIELD DID STOP WILLIE STARGELL FROM JOINING THE 500 HOME RUN CLUB

In 1946, young phenom Ralph Kiner cracked 23 home runs to lead the league, but only 8 of those cleared the fences at home. The team was hoping to sign aging slugger Hank Greenberg, but he didn't want to come to Pittsburgh, where homers went to die. It took three things to get him: $100,000 (roughly $1.4 million today), a Thoroughbred horse and a promise to shorten the fences.

An eight-foot-high fence was installed thirty feet in front of the existing left-field wall. And the home run fest began. Kiner would hit 51 and lead or co-lead the NL in homers every year he played at Forbes Field, averaging 45 per season. Greenberg, at age thirty-six, hit 25 homers—18 at home. Two years later, the fence was raised to sixteen feet.

Unfortunately, no adjustments were made for the next great Bucco slugger. Willie Stargell played six seasons at Forbes Field and was a top long-ball threat. But his numbers exploded at more hitter-friendly Three Rivers Stadium. In his first full season, he led the majors with 48 taters. Stargell finished his Hall-of-Fame career with 475. There's no question that playing at Forbes Field robbed him of at least 25 dingers.

IT WAS THE SITE OF HOLLYWOOD ON THE MON WAY BEFORE THE INDUSTRY MADE PITTSBURGH A REGULAR STOP

Forbes Field was the setting for 1951's *Angels in the Outfield*. The film, starring Paul Douglas, Janet Leigh and the underrated Keenan Wynn, was, according to IMDb, "the story of the brash and abusive manager of the Pittsburgh Pirates who receives the help of an angel to win games and become a better person in the process." As bad as the real Pirates were in the 1950s, who could blame a manager for being abusive?

IT HOSTED TWO BASEBALL ALL-STAR GAMES

The first Midsummer Classic at the stadium was in 1944, when Pirate hurler Rip Sewell tantalized AL hitters with his eephus pitch on the way to a 7–1

NL victory. In 1959, the game was expanded to a doubleheader to help fund the players' pension fund. The NL won, 5–4, with Pirates Bill Mazeroski, Elroy Face, Smoky Burgess and Dick Groat making the squad.

IT CLOSED MIDSEASON

In the late 1960s, the facility was starting to show its age. And Pitt was gobbling up Oakland as it looked to expand. But construction delays meant that the Pirates' new home, Three Rivers Stadium, wouldn't be ready to start the 1970 season. So, on June 28, in a bit of symmetry, the Bucs closed out Forbes Field as they opened it, with a win against the Cubs.

SITE OF THE ONLY WALK-OFF HOMER IN A GAME SEVEN

If the grand ballpark is known for one moment, it undoubtedly is Mazeroski's home run in the 1960 World Series. Leading off the bottom of the ninth and breaking a 9–9 tie in one of the wildest postseason games ever, Maz hit a homer that it remains the only walk-off home run in a game seven.

In one of the iconic photos in Pittsburgh sports history, Bill Mazeroski (*helmet off, in Pirate uniform on third base*) rounds third after hitting what remains the only walk-off game seven home run in World Series history. *Courtesy of the Pittsburgh Pirates.*

THERE ARE PARTS STILL AROUND

Forbes Field met the wrecking ball in 1971, but pieces of the facility still exist. To celebrate the anniversary of Maz's home run, each October 13, fans congregate in front of a remnant of Forbes Field's center-field wall on Roberto Clemente Drive to listen to a rebroadcast of game seven.

Another piece of Forbes Field can be found inside a building on Pitt's campus. In Wesley W. Posvar Hall, directly across from the wall, you'll find the last home plate used at Forbes Field encased in glass. Both remnants are reminders of a historic building that ushered in a new era of stadium construction.

2

AN ANNUAL LOVE AFFAIR WITH FORBES FIELD

By David Finoli

At 6:31 p.m. on June 28, 1970, sixty-one memory-filled years of Forbes Field came to an end. Shortstop Don Kessinger hit a ground ball to future Hall-of-Fame second baseman Bill Mazeroski. The Chicago Cubs' Willie Smith was on first base as Maz strolled over and tagged second base for the force-out that completed a doubleheader sweep for the Bucs, vaulting them into a tie for first place in the National League Eastern Division. The fact that they were on a seven-game winning streak or were in first place had little consequence on the perfect Pittsburgh afternoon. The essential point was that Mazeroski ending the ball game with a force-out brought down the curtain on Forbes Field.

It was appropriate that Maz made the final out, as he not only is arguably the greatest defensive second baseman in the history of the game but also had a hand in the most iconic moment of this treasured ballpark: the famed walk-off home run in the 1960 World Series that gave Pittsburgh its third world championship. As the June contest ended, some of the 40,918 fans who filled Forbes on this afternoon descended onto the playing field, forcing the legendary Bob Prince, who had been trying to announce the winners of baseball memorabilia from the field, into the dugout. The fans swarmed aggressively, trying to take whatever piece of the old place they could.

Over the next few months, a couple of fires were set in the ballpark, ignited by what investigators thought were young adults living in the facility. Finally, in July 1971, the inevitable happened. Forbes was demolished to

One of the unique things about Pittsburgh sports history is the fact that a portion of the Forbes Field was left up after the stadium was razed. Hundreds of fans gather at the wall every October 13 to hear the original broadcast of game seven of the 1960 World Series in another unique Pittsburgh sports tradition. *Courtesy of David Finoli.*

make way for a new building at the University of Pittsburgh, Posvar Hall. Luckily, someone had the foresight to leave a section of the wall up, a place where baseball fans could go to remember the incredible times they had at the first concrete and steel baseball stadium built in the National League.

Fast-forward fourteen years as a new baseball tradition began, very quietly and simply. It was an ode to this classic stadium and its most memorable moment. Saul Finkelstein lived in the Squirrel Hill district of Pittsburgh and reportedly was not having the best of days on October 13, 1985, when he decided to celebrate the twenty-fifth anniversary of Mazeroski's dramatic home run in a very interesting way. He took a cassette player and the tape of the game he owned, picked up a couple of hot dogs at the famed Oakland landmark the Original Hot Dog Shop and walked a couple of blocks to the flagpole at the Forbes Field wall and listened to the rebroadcast of the game. Every year until 1992 he did this by himself to commemorate the greatest game in Pirate history, starting at the same time the first pitch occurred and ending at 3:36 p.m., when Maz's famed home run went over Yogi Berra's head beyond the left-field wall.

In 1993, he went to the team's annual off-season celebration called PirateFest and saw a local author, Jim O'Brien, and told him about his annual trek to the wall. O'Brien, who had just written a book about the 1960 team, thought it was a great idea, even mentioning it on a local sports talk show. All of a sudden, Finkelstein was not alone on October 13. Many people decided to join him, to the point that it has become a must for many lifelong Pirate fans.

In 2010, a huge gathering was there, filling the space where the Forbes Field wall stands to celebrate the fiftieth anniversary of the moment. Eleven members of the 1960 team were there, along with many fans, listening to the pitch-by-pitch broadcast and screaming with joy when Mazeroski, who was also in attendance, once again hit his blast.

While it was unfortunately canceled in 2020 due to the COVID pandemic, the parade to the Forbes Field wall every October 13 has become a treasured tradition for Pirate fans, one that keeps the memory of this famed ballpark alive.

3

PHIL COYNE

Baseball's Only Hall-of-Fame Usher

By Dan Coyne

I t's safe to assume that Phil Coyne didn't have his sights set on Cooperstown
when he became an usher. And yet that's where you'll find his uniform
and ID badge, set among a collection of Pirate memorabilia. It seems
improbable, but only if you'd never met him.

Proximity and luck brought "Philly" to Forbes Field. Born in 1918, he
grew up on Halket Street, a ten-minute walk from the ballpark. One of
his neighbors was a policeman who worked at a patrol station on Forbes
Avenue, next to Gus Miller's newsstand. Gus was, for many years, the head
usher at Forbes Field. His corner newsstand buzzed with activity like a
scene from *On the Waterfront* but with ushers, not longshoremen, looking for
work. The policeman put in a good word with Gus, and that's how Philly
became an usher. He was eighteen. It was 1936. His first post was on a
ramp in right field.

Fast-forward about eighty years. Philly is ninety-nine and still working
games. His spare rags—the only tools of the trade—are stuffed in a blue
plastic bag that he keeps on a concrete ledge that frames the back of his
section, near third base. He's got a soft rag in one hand as he waits for
customers. Leaning against a railing, he radiates warmth. Everything about
him is genuine. He really *is* that happy to see you.

By this point, his story has spread. He's been profiled in newspapers and
on TV—the man who, as a young fan, saw Babe Ruth hit his last three
home runs and, as an usher, saw Bill Mazeroski hit his walk-off homer in

Pictured to the left is legendary Pittsburgh Pirate usher Phil Coyne. Phil's career with the team lasted 81 years before he retired shortly before his 100th birthday in 2018. He had the honor of having his ID badge, Pirate cap and polo shirt put permanently on display at the National Baseball Hall of Fame. Sadly, he passed away in 2021 at the age of 102. *Courtesy of Dan Coyne.*

game seven. He was also featured, memorably, in a live cutaway during the 2013 National League East Wild Card game. "Will you be back next year?" the interviewer asked. "As long as my mind don't take me to the football field when I'm supposed to be at the baseball field," the ninety-five-year-old quipped. (Philly also ushered Steeler and Pitt football games, sometimes working all three in a matter of days.)

Philly stayed at PNC Park for four more years before retiring. He knew it'd be nice to make it to one hundred as an usher, but his legs were losing their strength. The Pirates would have found a place for him, something comfortable. But that wasn't his style.

As impressive as Philly's tenure was, longevity doesn't explain why he was so adored—or why the Pirates, at his retirement, mounted a plaque honoring him in his section. It was his character. To know Philly was to understand the meaning of kindness, decency and dedication. His sense of duty—of doing the right thing by others—was profound.

He was drafted into the U.S. Army in May 1941. He wouldn't return to ushering baseball games until 1946. The years between found him training in Mississippi and Oklahoma, on maneuvers in Louisiana and, eventually, on a troop ship, the SS *Santa Rosa*, heading to Africa. His unit, the 939th Field Artillery Battalion, made an overland march across North Africa before crossing the sea to Italy. That was where Philly endured his first aerial bombardment, near Naples. At war's end, he was in Germany. "This concluded 517 combat days for the Battalion," his unit's history coolly noted.

Philly returned to a job at Westinghouse Air Brake in Wilmerding, just outside of Pittsburgh. He earned sixty-five cents an hour as a machinist making couplings for railcars. He worked there for three decades, always taking his pay straight to his mother. Philly was a lifelong bachelor and spent most of his life in the same house on Halket Street.

When the Pirates had a night game at Forbes Field, he'd finish his shift in Wilmerding, take two streetcars back to Oakland, change clothes and walk to the ballpark. He'd bring his tips home—piles of nickels and dimes. His mother could tell, from the sound of the coins hitting the kitchen table, if he'd stopped at a bar on the way home.

Philly died just a few weeks shy of turning 103. The turnout at his funeral was more befitting a celebrity than a machinist from Oakland who made a name for himself cleaning seats and greeting people, many of them strangers, with a smile. He never took anything for granted—the ballpark, the fans, the Phil Coyne baseball card issued by Topps. He appreciated all of it, just as much as everyone appreciated him.

*Dan Coyne was Phil Coyne's nephew and a frequent visitor to his section in PNC Park.

4

IN THE SHADOW OF MAZ'S HOME RUN

By David Finoli

A t 3:36 p.m. on October 13, 1960, Pirate second baseman Bill Mazeroski launched a ball over the left-field wall of Forbes Field to give Pittsburgh its third World Series championship with an exciting 10–9 victory over the powerful New York Yankees in game seven of the Fall Classic. Sixty-plus years later, it remains the only game seven walk-off home run in World Series history. To say it was the greatest moment in Pirate history is a vast understatement. There isn't anything close.

So, in the more than six decades since that magical moment, what has Maz's home run left in its wake? First, in team history, it cost two other players the distinction of having the greatest hit in franchise history.

In 1925, the Bucs had dropped three of the first four games to the defending world champion Washington Senators. Only one loss from a series defeat, Pittsburgh captured games five and six to tie the Fall Classic and send it to a seventh and deciding game on a very rainy day at Forbes Field. Down at one point, 6–3, the Bucs battled back to tie the game, 6–6, in the seventh inning. Washington went ahead in the top of the eighth before Carson Bigbee tied the score with a double to left in the bottom of the eighth. Later in the frame, with two outs and the bases loaded, Hall of Famer Kiki Cuyler came to the plate and lashed a hit that saw the ball end up under the tarp in right field for a ground rule double that gave Pittsburgh the two winning runs in a 9–7 win for world championship number two.

Danny Murtaugh (*left*) and catcher Hal Smith (*right*) celebrate after capturing the 1960 World Series. If not for Bill Mazeroski's walk-off home run in the ninth, Smith's shot in the bottom of the eighth, which gave Pittsburgh a temporary 9–7 lead, would have been remembered as the greatest home run in franchise history. *Courtesy of the Pittsburgh Pirates.*

Thirty-five years later, in the eighth inning of the seventh game of the 1960 series, a reserve catcher by the name of Hal Smith smacked a three-run homer that also gave the Pirates a 9–7 lead and most likely the world championship. The only problem in this scenario was that New York scratched out two runs in the top of the ninth to tie the game. Moments later, Maz hit his legendary home run that made Hal Smith an afterthought in franchise history.

Leaving Cuyler and Smith in his dust was only one factor of the long ball that is still commemorated with a statue at PNC Park and a plaque on a sidewalk in Oakland where the ball flew over for the dramatic win. It also launched a debate, arguably a senseless one, as to who hit the greatest homer in baseball history. Some of the contenders to Mazeroski include:

- Game six of the 1991 World Series, when Kirby Puckett smashed a long ball to send it to a seventh and deciding game. This one isn't even in the same realm of a walk-off game seven World Series homer.
- Bucky "Bleeping" Dent's homer in the 1978 AL East deciding game. It wasn't a walk-off. Enough bleeping said

- Barry Bonds hitting his 756th home run, or Mark McGwire smacking his 62nd or 70th. Both were tainted by the steroid era.
- Joe Carter ending the 1993 series with a home run. Close, but it was only a sixth game. The Blue Jays would have had another chance the next day had they lost.
- The Carlton Fisk 1975 game six homer. It was dramatic, but Boston lost the series a night later. Advantage Maz.
- An injured Kirk Gibson winning game one of the 1988 Fall Classic. It was exciting, but it was only game one.
- Hank Aaron breaking the Babe's record. A more serious contender than McGwire or Bonds, but it didn't win a world championship.
- The "shot heard 'round the world." The Giants came from thirteen games back to force a three-game playoff against the Brooklyn Dodgers in 1951. Tied at one game apiece and Brooklyn entering the bottom of the ninth with a 4–1 lead, which soon was cut to 4–2, Bobby Thompson hit a three-run homer down a short 279-foot left-field line to give the Giants a 5-4 win and the National League pennant.

Thompson's homer is the one most argued about, while the Mazeroski shot is the greatest. It is worth noting here that the Giants lost the World Series to the Yankees and the 1951 Giants season was shrouded in a sign-stealing controversy. The bottom line: Bill Mazeroski's home run ended a World Series in the seventh and final game, lifting a huge underdog to a victory over the mighty New York Yankees. Just as there is no moment in franchise history that comes close to equaling the greatness of the hit, there is no home run in major league history that comes close. Debate ended.

5

A SEASON OF INEPTITUDE

The 1967 Pittsburgh Phantoms

By David Finoli

When a team like the Pittsburgh Phantoms are mentioned in the city's sports lore, a low-budget, minor league organization is the first thing that comes to mind. If that is your thought process, I have a story for you.

Born out of the excitement that came with the 1966 World Cup victory by England, the National Professional Soccer League (NPSL) was born. Pittsburgh was one of ten cities chosen to host a team. The team, named the Phantoms, played its home games at Forbes Field. Over the course of the year, the team bought several European stars, employed no fewer than four head coaches, had a Steinbrennerian owner and, remarkably, almost brought down the new NHL franchise, the Penguins, in the process. They did this all with a last-place effort in their one season.

Peter H. Block and Dick George were investors in the city's new NHL team, the Pittsburgh Penguins, and brought on other investors in a twenty-man group to purchase Pittsburgh's entry into the NPSL. The first order of business was to hire a coach and general manager. This was Herb Vogt, who was entrusted with putting together a squad. Vogt went through Europe looking for talent. He built a team and had Block and George travel overseas to get a glimpse of what he had assembled.

Not long after they reached Europe, the two men, unfortunately, learned that Vogt was having health issues and was advised by his doctors to resign from his position as Phantoms coach. Block was confident he'd have a coach in place within days and was also ready to announce the team's first signing, which the press was told would be a player of some note in Europe. The Phantoms' president announced that he had signed Budapest native Janos Bedl as his coach, and his first two player acquisitions were Dutch star Co Prins, who starred for the legendary Ajax squad, and Jürgen Klein, a twenty-three-year-old from Germany. After he signed, Jürgen decided to stay in Germany for a while and didn't fly over to the States until the season was about to begin.

Block also told the crowd he had hired Europe's top player agent, Raymond Schwab, as director of player personnel to secure the Phantoms more talent. Schwab quickly put together the rest of the seventeen-man squad, which Schwab claimed was one of the best in the world. Signing Prins was met with such an uproar in Holland, as was inking defenseman Pieter De Groot from Sparta, that the country's parliament quickly gathered to see about enacting a law that would forbid American representatives from talking to or signing the nation's players.

The team began its existence by training in Essen, Germany, on February 1, before coming back to Pittsburgh, where it continued season preparations at the South Park Fairgrounds and then Moon High School's football stadium. It was there where problems began. It turned out to be an unusually early spring, as bad weather and heavy snow interrupted spring training on several occasions. In a scrimmage in less-than-ideal weather, Prins injured his groin and German winger Manfred Seissler hurt his knee. Eventually, the team went to Atlanta to continue practice, but, while there was no snow, the players complained about the heat—only seventy-four degrees. The team eventually returned to Pittsburgh.

As the beginning of the season neared, changes continued to be made in the front office. Schwab decided to return to Europe and was replaced by Ted DeGroot. The team began the year on a California road trip, where, led by Prins, they tied the California Clippers and Los Angeles Toros before coming home to Forbes Field to face the Toronto Falcons. The home opener was rained out, and the Phantoms had to wait an evening to beat Toronto, 4–3, on a cold April night in front of a boisterous crowd of 6,359 to take the eastern division lead with twenty points. (The NPSL had a strange scoring system, with six points for a win, three for a tie and one bonus point for each of a team's first three goals.)

The win over the Falcons proved to be the calm before the storm. They lost their next game to St. Louis, 4–1, prompting Block to bring out his Steinbrenner side, firing Bedl after four games. Block claimed in a *Pittsburgh*

Post-Gazette article on May 2, 1967, that Bedl "wasn't coaching the team" and that "there was no instructional strategy." All this despite the fact that the team was in first place. He put Prins temporarily in charge as coach, and he immediately led them to a 5–3 win at Baltimore. Then the wheels fell off. They hired their fourth coach, Pepi Gruber, as the team tumbled from first to last place.

While Block continued to sign high-priced talent, including three Brazilian stars in August, the Phantoms continued to struggle and finished the season 10-14-7, in last place. Financially, the season was a disaster. They had to settle with Bedl, eventually paying him $32,500. They signed another Sparta player, Theo Laseroms, who apparently was still under contract to his former team. This cost the Phantoms another $50,000 in a settlement. They averaged just 3,068 fans per game to Forbes Field, and as it turned out, Schwab was signing the players at an elevated price and overcharging the Phantoms for their services. Altogether, the team lost $750,000 at a time when that was a huge amount.

Months later, the league merged with the United Soccer Association to form the North American Soccer League (NASL). The Phantoms were left out of the group going forward. The team, a financial failure, was disbanded after one season.

So bad were the losses that Block, who was given credit for coming up with the idea to petition the NHL to have a team in Pittsburgh in the 1967 NHL expansion, and the rest of the Pittsburgh Penguin ownership group had to sell their stake in the Penguins in only the third year of the franchise's existence to the Donald Parsons Group.

So, in the long run, the Pittsburgh Phantoms was more than just a minor league club. It was a lesson in how inept management can spend so much money and cause such damage in its wake.

6

FACE'S LAST STAND

By David Finoli

Franchises honor their great players in many ways. Statues, retired numbers, induction into their Halls of Fame. On August 31, 1968, after selling him to the Detroit Tigers for a reported $100,000, Pittsburgh honored the man who is still considered their greatest reliever, Roy Face, in a unique way. They let him throw one pitch in his final contest as a Pirate to set the all-time major league record for games pitched in a career with one team before sending him on his way.

Roy Face was a Renaissance man for sure over his career with the Bucs. In an era when relievers were mainly secondary pitchers if the starters tired out, Roy was in the game as part of a winning strategy. He was a quality pitcher who was brought in for clutch situations. He spent fifteen years in a Pittsburgh uniform, winning exactly 100 games, saving another 186. In his historic season, 1959, he was a remarkable 18-1 for a team that finished only 2 games over .500. (At the time of his retirement his 191 career saves, after he collected 5 more with the expansion Montreal Expos in 1969, was second all-time behind Hoyt Wilhelm.)

The 1962 Fireman of the Year in the National League was still pitching effectively in 1968, but he was forty years old and not in the long-range plans of the club. The Detroit Tigers were leading the American League pennant race, but the Baltimore Orioles had cut into their lead. Face was having a decent season despite his age, with 13 saves and a 2.60 ERA. Detroit wanted veteran bullpen help, so they arranged to purchase him from the Bucs for

Roy Face (*left*) helped redefine the role of the reliever in baseball. Before being sold to the Detroit Tigers in 1968, he pitched to one more batter in a Pirate uniform so he could tie Walter Johnson's major league mark of 802 games for one team. He also held the all-time record of games pitched in the National League, a record that stood until Kent Tekulve topped it in 1986, and he held the saves record in the senior circuit, broken by Bruce Sutter in 1982. *Courtesy of the Pittsburgh Pirates.*

$100,000. The deal couldn't be completed until September 1, because Detroit would not have a roster spot open until that point, when clubs could expand to forty players. In a quote from the *Pittsburgh Press* in the September 1, 1968 edition, general manager Joe L. Brown stated: "We have many problems. Face will be 41 next year and we have the expansion draft coming up and we must decide whether we want to protect the younger fellows."

As August was ending and his time in Pittsburgh was coming to an end, Face was 1 game short of tying Walter Johnson's major league record of 802 games pitched with one team. With one day left before the deal officially took place, Pittsburgh wanted him to start the August 31 contest against the Atlanta Braves then leave after one batter to tie the mark. Not knowing he had been traded, Face told management that he preferred to equal the mark the same way that he had pitched most of his 801 games at that point: in relief.

The game started in front of a small crowd of 4,671 at Forbes. No one in the stands knew this would be the final contest in a Pirate uniform for the heralded reliever. Steve Blass started the contest, retiring center fielder Felipe Alou to lead off the first inning. He then surprisingly went to left field to replace Carl Taylor, as manager Larry Shepard brought Face into the contest. Roy, who was confused when asked to warm up, threw one pitch to second baseman Felix Millan, forcing him to ground out. Shepard then emerged from the dugout to walk Face off the mound. Face had officially tied Johnson's mark. He said he had no idea what was going on, "but then I heard rumors. An usher told me, then another and I began to wonder [apparently in an era when ushers heard rumors before the press]."

Blass returned to the mound, as pinch-hitting legend Manny Mota replaced him in left. The reliever walked into the locker room, where Brown gave him the official news. Face was sad to leave but was at least happy he was going to a contender, even though he would be ineligible for the World Series. "It's a fine break for me and a sad moment too."

As sad as it was, it was a unique way to honor a player and one of the most memorable moments in Forbes Field history.

7

FOR THE HEAVYWEIGHT CHAMPIONSHIP
OF THE WORLD

Ezzard Charles versus Joe Walcott

By Douglas Cavanaugh

The intentions of colorful Jake Mintz were pure. A proud Pittsburgher, he vowed that if he ever managed a heavyweight champion, he was going to give Pittsburgh its first heavyweight title bout, a huge thing in those days. So, when he became manager of Ezzard Charles and Ez won the title shortly after, Mintz made good on his word. It took a while, but he did it. And if he could give a payday to the popular but aging Jersey Joe Walcott along the way, so much the better.

The fight, the first heavyweight title bout in Pittsburgh history, was put together by the Rooney-McGinley Boxing Club. On July 18, 1951, a record crowd of 28,272 watched Walcott step into the ring at Forbes Field to face Charles. Former heavyweight champion Primo Carnera was at ringside, along with local fistic stars Billy Conn, Teddy Yarosz, Fritzie Zivic and Lee Sala and a legion of Pirate and Steeler players. Walcott was a 9-1 underdog, facing a champion who was 11-0 in Pittsburgh rings.

Charles and Walcott had fought twice before, Charles winning both by fifteen-round decision. Neither bout had been considered very exciting, but Charles had been a great favorite here for years, so having this contest in Pittsburgh was a smart move by everyone involved. This would be Walcott's fifth attempt to win the crown, his two bouts against Charles and his two losing tries against Joe Louis being the others.

But this night belonged to Jersey Joe, who, in round seven, walked into Charles and delivered a left hook–uppercut hybrid punch that nearly twisted Ezzard's head 180 degrees, easily one of the most brutally conclusive single punches in heavyweight title fight history. The champion crashed to the floor and remained there while referee Buck McTiernan tolled the terminal ten-count.

After so many hard years of struggle Walcott had finally won the big prize, becoming the oldest man to ascend to the heavyweight championship (a distinction he held for forty-three years until George Foreman turned the trick at age forty-five). The tearful old fighter won the hearts of the entire nation with his Cinderella-story victory. He was front-page news everywhere. Jackie Robinson wired his congratulations to Joe, stating, "I wish I had your power." *The Ring* magazine later awarded the bout its "Fight of the Year" for 1951.

Incidentally, Art Rooney almost missed the chance to be a part of this memorable event. Earlier that year, he had quit the fight game when Steelers general manager John Holahan was named athletic commissioner for West PA. Rooney felt that might be viewed as a conflict of interest. As fate would have it, Holahan resigned his post with the Steelers a month before the Walcott-Charles fight, allowing Art to rejoin his promotional team and make boxing history.

After the bout, Bob Baker, a large, skilled and fast-rising local heavyweight hopeful, was seen approaching Walcott and whispering in his ear. When asked if he had challenged Jersey Joe for a first crack at the title, Baker responded, "No, thank you; man, you think I'm crazy?" Baker had wisdom beyond his tender years.

As for Jake Mintz, the man who made it all happen, one can only imagine his reaction behind the scenes. He fainted in the middle of the ring after Charles won the championship. It's a wonder he didn't have a coronary thrombosis after what Walcott did to Ezzard in round seven that night. The count of referee McTiernan must have been the longest, most painful ten seconds of Mintz's life.

8

ROONEY-McGINLEY BOXING CLUB

Bringing Fights to Oakland

By Douglas Cavanaugh

Why, we never even wait for our check when we fight for Rooney-McGinley. We just go back to Cincinnati and they send it to us. We have three more fights planned here and we hope we're always welcome. It's a pleasure to do business with high-class men.
—George Rhein, manager of Ezzard Charles

Johnny Kilbane marveled at hearing the business the Rooney-McGinley show will do here a week from Monday. He said it put Pittsburgh second only to New York as a current fighting center. He was right, too.
—Pittsburgh Press

I always said Pittsburgh was a great town. I've promised the Rooney-McGinley Co. I would fight in Pittsburgh this summer.
—Sugar Ray Robinson

The quotes above are just a few of the testimonies from the press and top-level fighters and managers as to the professionalism of the Rooney-McGinley Boxing Club. Boxing history is replete with promoters of questionable ethics, some even despised, like Don King, Mike Jacobs, Bob Arum and Tex Rickard. But you'd be hard-pressed to find anyone with anything negative to say about Art Rooney, Barney

McGinley or Jack McGinley. They were universally liked, respected and—most important—trusted.

Rooney dabbled in fight promotions years before joining forces with Barney McGinley, who had also been involved. The best in the business would come to Pittsburgh whenever they put on one of their boxing extravaganzas at Forbes Field. Whether local or from out of town, champion or challenger, a fighter almost always accepted the offer to be on a Rooney-McGinley card, because they knew they would be paid top dollar for their services and could expect to be dealt with fairly and honestly—an all-too-often rare thing in boxing.

Constant sniping and endless petty quarrels put Pittsburgh boxing in a precarious position by the summer of 1938. Honest, straight-ahead promoters like Jules Beck were pulling up stakes, leaving a lot of hungry opportunists to tear at the exposed remains. Commissioner William McClelland (nephew of the celebrated boxer Jack McClelland) was at war with Ray Foutts (manager of middleweight titlist Teddy Yarosz) over various things. Promoter Elwood Rigby had a huckster reputation and was making promises he couldn't keep, and he pretty much buried himself when he couldn't cover the money promised Billy Conn for one of his duels with Yarosz—a huge breach in ethics that cost him dearly. And hyper-verbal, scatterbrained Jake Mintz was at war with just about everybody, which didn't help his promotions very much.

The more established fighters at the time were largely unaffected, but promising up-and-comers like Billy Soose, who was about to make his hometown debut, were feeling the blowback from all the promotional fuss. Luckily for him and others, Pittsburgh Steeler moguls Rooney and McGinley would soon be launching their own promotional firm.

Rather than fight with rival promoters, Art and Barney instead often helped them in their endeavors, something fairly unprecedented at that time. They made use of the misdirected energies of Foutts and Mintz, making Ray their first matchmaker, followed by Jake shortly afterward. As a result, the Rooney-McGinley Boxing Club cleaned up a lot of the mess and kept things humming nicely for many years.

Art and Barney launched their promotional club with an inaugural fight card for the ages, featuring four world champions and two slayers of champions. The event took place at Forbes Field on July 17, 1939, and featured lightweight champion Sammy Angott, featherweight champion Petey Sarron, welterweight champion Fritzie Zivic, uncrowned champion Charley Burley, middleweight champion Teddy Yarosz and perennial light-heavyweight contender Al Gainer. It was intended as a showcase for the stars of the Pittsburgh fistic scene. The card drew 20,015 people, the second-largest crowd in Pittsburgh boxing history.

It was a memorable night for Pittsburgh sports, one of the most important in the city's sporting history.

9

STOP THE BALLGAME

Fans Listen to the Billy Conn–Joe Louis Fight
at Forbes Field Before the Pirate Game

David Finoli

While boxing fans may think that the closed-circuit, pay-per-view era in boxing began in the 1960s, its origins were at least a couple of decades earlier. Even though video wasn't available, fight fans in the Steel City gathered at Forbes Field on June 18, 1941, not just for a baseball game between their Buccos and the New York Giants, but also to listen to one of the great fights in the history of the sport. The heavyweight champion of the world, Joe Louis, was going up against arguably the most beloved boxer in the city's history, Billy Conn.

Born in Pittsburgh on October 8, 1917, Conn, nicknamed the "Pittsburgh Kid," made his Forbes Field debut on July 30, 1936, decisioning Teddy Movan in eight rounds. He fought at the home of the Pirates three more times before capturing the light-heavyweight championship of the world against Melio Bettina at Madison Square Garden in New York City. He defended his title three times, including a rematch against Bettina on September 25, 1939, before taking on some heavyweights in preparation to try to become the first light-heavyweight champion to capture the heavyweight crown. He would earn that opportunity two years later at the Polo Grounds in New York against arguably the greatest fighter ever to win the heavyweight title, Joe Louis.

Fight fans in Pittsburgh were ecstatic about the opportunity to see their hero attempt to make history. The Pirates were having a decent season in

Almost twenty-five thousand people showed up at Forbes Field on June 18, 1941, to hear the radio broadcast of hometown star Billy Conn (*pictured*) taking on heavyweight champion Joe Louis, along with seeing the Pirate game that evening. Leading on the scorecards going into the thirteenth round, Conn decided to go for a knockout rather than continuing his boxing mastery over Louis. The champion ended up knocking out Conn and retaining his title. *Courtesy of the Conn Family.*

1941, but certainly not a pennant-contending one, and they stood at 21-27 when the game began. In what would be the last season during World War II when most of the game's greats were available to play on the major league diamonds before going off to war, the Bucs were not drawing well. They saw the opportunity to lure fans to Forbes Field by broadcasting the fight from New York over the loudspeakers at the famed stadium before the Pirate-Giant contest.

The promotion worked, as a season-high crowd to that point of 24,738 fans (it ended up as the third-biggest of the year at Forbes) showed up at the Oakland facility. They were treated to a great evening of sports. The baseball game began with the Bucs plating two in the opening inning when right fielder Bob Elliott tripled in Lee Handley and Frankie Gustine in the bottom of the first. The Pirates' Max Butcher was on the mound pitching brilliantly, giving up only a run in the second and another in the fourth. After New York's Ken O'Day grounded out to Gustine to end the fourth, the game stopped and the fight that no self-respecting Pittsburgh sports fan would want to miss began to play over the PA system.

Joe Louis was a prohibitive favorite in a contest that many felt would end relatively quickly. Conn was twenty-five pounds lighter than the champion but was quick and one of the best defensive boxers of his era. The challenger was fighting brilliantly, jabbing and moving, and Louis was having trouble. Louis finally caught him in the fifth with a savage shot, but Conn came back and was beating the champion to the punch, building up a lead that stunned the crowd at Forbes Field.

The joyous throng was listening to what was turning out to be the greatest upset in heavyweight history, but as the story goes, Billy Conn got a little too cocky and tried to end the fight early instead of continuing to box and move after hurting the champ in the twelfth. Louis took advantage and pounded Conn until he was down for the count, ending the fight a round later with his championship still intact.

Twenty-five thousand disappointed fans still had the remainder of the baseball game to watch following the broadcast. It was an interesting contest, as the score remained tied at the end of nine, 2–2, and continued tied through eleven innings when the game was called because of the National League curfew of 1:00 a.m.

The Pirates rebounded to finish the year with an 81-73 mark, and the game would be replayed later that season. But on June 18, the frustrated crowd went home on a night that had begun full of hope.

10

JOSH GIBSON

The Greatest of All Forbes Field Hitters

By Thomas Kern

The hallowed grounds of Forbes Field, situated in the city's Oakland neighborhood, showcased many a Pittsburgh talent from its opening in 1909 through its last game in 1970.

Honus Wagner, Pie Traynor, the Waners, Ralph Kiner, Roberto Clemente and Willie Stargell were Pittsburgh Pirate greats. But a case can be made that the greatest Pittsburgh hitter to display his flair at Forbes Field was Josh Gibson. Gibson did not play for the Pirates. Not that he wasn't good enough to do so. Baseball's version of Jim Crow kept him in the Negro Leagues for his entire career.

Josh was born on December 21, 1911, in Buena Vista, Georgia. His father sought work in the North as part of the Great Migration in the early 1900s. After he found employment in the Pittsburgh steel mills, he relocated his family in 1923.

Growing up, Josh loved sports, but he loved baseball best and soon found a home on a semipro team called the Pittsburgh Crawford Giants. The Crawfords would become one of the premier Negro League teams in the 1930s. But it was with the Homestead Grays that Gibson first became known, debuting with the Grays on July 25, 1930, in a night game against the Kansas City Monarchs played under the Monarchs' portable lighting system. That game was at Forbes Field. Famously called out of the stands to play when Homestead catcher Buck Ewing was injured, Josh would play more games at Forbes than at any other National or American League park.

Seen jogging to home plate is one of the greatest hitters the game has ever known, Josh Gibson. One of the most important players on the championship teams the Pittsburgh Crawfords and Homestead Grays produced, Gibson is arguably the greatest hitter in Negro League history. *Courtesy of the Pittsburgh Pirates.*

Gibson finished out the 1930 season platooning with Ewing and then took over the catching reins full time in 1931. That Homestead squad is considered one of the greatest Negro League teams ever. Gibson was only nineteen, but his hitting was already impressive. In that 1931 season, in which the Grays played a number of its home games at Forbes, Josh hit .311 with a slugging percentage of .563 and a very respectable on-base plus slugging percentage (OPS) of .923.

The Grays lost Gibson back to the Crawfords in 1932, when he signed a more lucrative contract than Homestead owner Cumberland Posey could offer. That stretch with the Crawfords (1932–36) saw Gibson emerge as a star. In 1937, faced with financial difficulties, the Crawfords traded Josh back to Homestead, where he would play for the next ten years until his untimely death in January 1947. Homestead had its own field in Pittsburgh but often arranged games at Forbes Field. This suited the Grays well, allowing them to play prime opponents and draw a bigger gate.

Forbes Field was a cavernous ballpark. Its dimensions in 1930 were 365 feet to the left-field corner, 457 at the deepest corner of the park,

435 to center and 300 (in 1925) in right. However, as large as it was, it could not contain Gibson. His Forbes Field homers are the stuff of legend. And when he was not hitting homers, he took advantage of the outfield expanse, collecting extra-base hits. The right-handed Gibson was famous for his muscular arms and shoulders. In baseball parlance, he could turn on the ball, pulling it to left field. Yet he was equally able to hit the ball to all fields and play the gaps at Forbes.

His twelve-year tenure with Homestead, involving a significant number of home games at Forbes, yielded a .364 batting average, .451 on-base percentage, .694 slugging percentage and an OPS of 1.145. Stories of Josh's exploits expand on these numbers. In September 1930, his debut year, during the Grays' postseason series with the Lincoln Giants, Gibson attained legendary status. In the second game of a doubleheader at Forbes, he cleared the 457-foot left-center-field fence and tripled in a 17–16 Homestead victory. The September 27, 1930 *Pittsburgh Courier* carried columnist W. Rollo Wilson's recap of the game. "Gibson is green but a terrific threat when crouching over the plate with a bat…his homer and triple in Pittsburgh were mighty wallops." Records show that only two big leaguers, Mickey Mantle and Dick Stuart, accomplished this feat. And Josh did it twice.

Tragically, Gibson suffered an early death on January 20, 1947, after a multiyear struggle with a brain tumor and complications from it. Jackie Robinson broke the color barrier only a few months later. Several years before, Pirate president William Benswanger allegedly considered giving tryouts to Negro League ballplayers. Local writers lauded Gibson as the top player to consider, but nothing came of it. Had Josh lived, as the game's integration slowly began, he might well have finally been signed by the Pirates to bolster their lineup and provide an opportunity for all baseball fans to see how great he was.

11

A PANDEMIC CONTEST TO REMEMBER

Pitt Crushes Defending National Champion Georgia Tech

By David Finoli

As we enter the third decade of the twenty-first century, the one news story that has almost completely overshadowed everything else is the COVID-19 pandemic. It has affected just about everything we do in life, including the sports world. Games have been canceled, and many contests and events have been severely limited in attendance, even to the point that fans have not been allowed in the facilities during the games. The pandemic has been often referred to as unprecedented. It's been horrible, certainly, but unprecedented it is not.

In 1918, the world was suffering through a pandemic. The Spanish flu epidemic affected over 500 million people. It was so bad that 675,000 people died in this country alone. Add to the fact that while it was coming to an end, World War I was still going on in Europe. As it did in 2020, the pandemic of 1918 had an effect on the sports world. Major League Baseball had a shortened season, and the nation's other major sport, college football, had more than half of its season cut. The University of Pittsburgh football squad, one of the best in the nation, would play only five contests, including a season-ending game against the Cleveland Naval Reserve. One of their games was against the defending national champions, a team thought to be so powerful that even the Panthers had little hope for victory: the Golden Tornedo of Georgia Tech.

One of the greatest coaches in the history of the game, Glenn Scobey "Pop" Warner came to Pitt in 1915 and immediately took the program to national prominence. He went 60-12-4 and led the school to three national titles in his first four seasons with the Panthers. *Courtesy of the University of Pittsburgh Athletics.*

Pitt, led by legendary coach Glenn Scobey "Pop" Warner, opened the season with dominant wins over Washington and Jefferson, 34–0, and the University of Pennsylvania, 37–0. Both were at Forbes Field and showed just how good Warner's team was. These were fine showings, but taking on their next opponent, Georgia Tech, would be a whole different experience.

The Golden Tornado, as the team was called at the time, was led by coach John Heisman—yes, the man for whom the famed award is named. Heisman was an innovator, featuring the forward pass in his famed jump-shift offense at a time when most coaches preferred the more conventional, violent, up-the-middle running offense—the "three yards and a cloud of dust" approach, if you will. The results were remarkable. They outscored their opponents 491–17 in their undefeated 1917 schedule, winning the national championship in the process. A year later, their defense wasn't scored on in their first five games, while the offense scored 425 points, including breaking the century mark against Furman (118–0), Georgia Eleventh Calvary (123–0) and N.C. State (128–0). Pitt was to play Syracuse on November 23 in a rescheduled contest from earlier in the year, but Warner wanted to play the best and convinced Georgia Tech to come to Forbes Field. Was this move stupid or shrewd? By nightfall of this day, it would turn out to be very shrewd.

Heisman was a Hall-of-Fame coach, but while the college football world expected yet another rout, Warner showed why he is considered one of the all-time best.

In a stunning development, the Pitt defense proved to be superior to the legendary Tech offense, limiting it to just 18 yards rushing and 0 passing. The Panthers' R.A. Easterday hit Tom Davies for a 20-yard scoring strike to vault ahead, 7–0. Davies then returned a punt 50 yards to double Pitt's lead before the two connected again on a 35-yard touchdown toss to put Pitt up 20–0 early in the third quarter.

Would Heisman figure out a way to get his team charged to mount a comeback? The answer was no. Pitt ended up scoring two more times, including Davies's fourth touchdown on a 55-yard run to cap a convincing 32–0 rout. The college football world couldn't believe it. The offense that couldn't be stopped had been stopped cold.

With the win, the Panthers went on to capture their third national title in this pandemic year. It was arguably their greatest win while playing at Forbes Field.

12

OF STEAGLES AND CARPITTS

The Steelers Make Their Way through World War II at Forbes Field

By David Finoli

Imagine if you will the stars of the NFL not being able to play because they had to serve their country during wartime. A game without Cam Heyward or Patrick Mahomes. It's hard to imagine such a scenario. But this is what happened during World War II. The vast majority of Major League Baseball and National Football League players went off to war, leaving the game to those who were either too young or old to fight or had acquired 4F status, men who had disabilities that prevented them from being drafted. For the sport of professional football, it almost proved to be its undoing.

The NFL's Brooklyn Dodgers had no players as the 1943 season approached, and the Steelers could pull together only six. Pittsburgh's cross-state brethren, the Philadelphia Eagles, were also struggling to find players. So, to survive, the two teams merged, as did Brooklyn and Boston a year later. In Pennsylvania, the new amalgamation was called the Pittsburgh-Philadelphia Steagles. The black and gold of the Steelers was changed to green and white for a season. In an article on philadelphiaeagles.com by Ray Didinger, Steeler owner Art "The Chief" Rooney stated: "It was done out of necessity. The war was going on and most of the players were in the service. A lot of coaches too. We didn't have the manpower to field a team and neither did the Eagles, but we thought we could make it work if we pulled our resources."

The team that split its games between Shibe Park in Philadelphia and Forbes Field was a combination of two franchises that had enjoyed little success in their short NFL histories to that point. Pittsburgh was coming off its first winning season with a 7-4 mark in 1942; the Eagles had never had a winning record. As the Chief stated, they needed to pool their resources, and that included making Pittsburgh head man Walt Kiesling and Philadelphia's Greasy Neale co-coaches, with Kiesling heading up the defense and Neale the offense. Both men were headstrong, and it was a season full of head-coaching battles. The team included a center who couldn't hear out of one ear and a receiver who was partially blind.

Somehow, through all the arguments and roster issues, the team played over .500, finishing with a 5-4-1 mark. That record included victories in the team's only two contests at Forbes Field, a 34–13 win against the Chicago Cardinals and a 35–34 nail-biter against the Detroit Lions.

For the Eagles, it was the beginning of a championship era, as they were able to field a team on their own the next season, finishing 7-1-2 and eventually winning their first two league championships, in 1948 and 1949. For Pittsburgh, times were still tough, and Rooney was forced to combine with another team in 1944, the Chicago Cardinals. This team would be referred to as the Car-Pitts. As it turned out, it was an appropriate name.

There was little talent on the Chicago roster. The team was coming off of a winless 0-10-0 campaign. Adding the Steelers to their team didn't improve the situation. In an Associated Press article on ESPN.com, Car-Pitt lineman Chet Bulger said, "We were terrible. You'd get beat so bad you'd cry." The numbers back him up. They were outscored 32.8–10.8 points per game, and this was after a close 30–28 loss to the Cleveland Rams in the opener, a game that gave them a false sense of security for the season. Losing 34–7 at Green Bay the next week took that away. The team tossed 41 interceptions, and their 32.7 yards per punt is still an NFL low.

The amalgamation ended up 0-10-0 and is considered one of the worst teams to take the field in league history. In 1945, the dual-team experiment ended as the players began to return from overseas and the game began to turn normal again. While many mock the Steagles and the Car-Pitts, author Matthew Algeo in his book *Last Team Standing* said it best: "These men—known sometimes derisively, as 4-F's—kept the NFL alive....They didn't storm the beaches of Iwo Jima or Normandy. They couldn't. But they were, in smaller ways, heroic. In America's darkest hours, they gave the nation something to cheer about, and their accomplishments, often in the face of long odds, exemplified the spirit that won the war." It is why we should always remember fondly those who played for the Steagles and Car-Pitts.

13

DON'T TAKE ANYONE FOR GRANTED

Carnegie Tech Stuns Knute Rockne and His Irish of Notre Dame

By David Finoli

I t's a rule all coaches preach: don't take anyone for granted. Even Pitt coaches Paul Hackett and Dave Hart pressed the importance of that to their teams. (Although, let's face it, there were few teams in the Hackett and Hart eras that they could actually take for granted, but I digress). While it's an age-old philosophy, on November 28, 1926, when the powerful Notre Dame Fighting Irish came to Forbes Field to face the Carnegie Tech Tartans, it was one that the visitors didn't exactly take to heart.

The Irish were coming into this contest at 8-0 and looking to be a strong favorite to capture head coach Knute Rockne's second national championship in three seasons. Walter Steffen's Tartans were enjoying a fine season at 6-2 but were 5-to-1 underdogs in this contest and had been outscored by Notre Dame 111–19 in the previous four meetings between the two teams. So there weren't many who expected this to go in the home team's favor. Still, you don't take any opponent for granted. Right, Knute? Knute?

Apparently, Rockne had another rule: don't take anyone for granted… unless you've outscored them 111–19 in four games, then apparently it's OK. First, the Notre Dame coach wanted to keep his first team at home in order to keep them fresh for the season finale against USC. After all, against one of the toughest schedules in the nation he had outscored his opponents in four contests by a 197–7 margin. Certainly the second team could handle Carnegie Tech. Under pressure, he relented and assured the officials at Tech that he would send the first team to Pittsburgh to play the Tartans, but they would travel to the Steel City without their head coach. While Rockne sent his team, he chose not to send himself, deciding to stay back in Chicago to attend the Western Conference college coaches meeting. Well, that was partly true. He actually decided not to go so that he could attend the Army-Navy game in the Windy City. He had a contract to write an article about the contest that would appear in newspapers around the country. Suffice it to say, having any form of respect for his opponent that week had gone out the window.

A record crowd of forty-five thousand jammed into every nook and cranny of Forbes Field to see the powerful Fighting Irish, now led by Knute's assistant, Heartley "Hunk" Anderson. Somehow, a coach named Hunk didn't have the same flair as one named Knute, but the Irish were still going to steamroll the Tartans. If they had, maybe Ronald Reagan would have played Hunk Anderson in the movie about Rockne's life, *Knute Rockne, All American*, instead of George Gipp. What was about to transpire on the gridiron at Forbes over the next few hours was so embarrassing to the program that, needless to say, the screenwriters made sure they left it out of the memorable film.

Steffen's squad dominated the game from the onset. He inspired his club, saying, "Men, Knute Rockne thinks you are so poor as football players that he's starting his second string against you, and he's so sure he'll win, he's not even here. He's in Chicago watching Army and Navy play some real football." Anderson started the second team, and the Tartans made him pay for it. They controlled the game, but it wasn't until Anderson inserted the first team into the game that Tech scored. A 13-yard run by Bill Donahue, followed by a 1-yard burst by Cyril J. Letzelter, gave the Tartans a stunning 13–0 lead at the half.

A funny thing happened in the second half. While most people expected the Irish to wake up and grab control of the game, two Howard Harpster field goals were all the points scored. Notre Dame was humbled on this day, 19–0, in a game ESPN ranked as was the third-greatest upset in the history of the sport.

It was certainly a humble moment for the great coach. Going forward in his legendary career, Knute Rockne would live the coaching philosophy of never taking a team for granted.

II

PITT STADIUM
(1925–1999)

14

IN THE SHADOW OF
THE CATHEDRAL OF LEARNING

The History of Pitt Stadium

By David Finoli

Even as baseball was finally becoming popular again after the embarrassment of the 1919 World Series, college football was its equal in the eyes of the American sports fan. It was perhaps even more popular. It was becoming in vogue for universities to build mammoth new stadiums to satisfy the many faithful who wanted to spend Saturday afternoons cheering on their local school. The University of Pittsburgh was no different. It had seemingly outgrown Forbes Field and was intent on building a behemoth of a facility on campus. The school had won three national championships under the legendary Glenn "Pop" Warner in the preceding decade and felt that an on-campus stadium was the next step in keeping the program elite. The university chose a site and built a facility more elaborate than what it had started to construct, at the same time that the powers that be at Pitt were focused on their project, which would become the landmark on campus: the Cathedral of Learning.

John Gabbert Bowman, selected as the university's tenth chancellor in 1921, was focused on the construction of what would become the single greatest landmark on campus as well as one of the most renowned collegiate buildings in the country. While Bowman was putting his efforts into the Cathedral of Learning, the school had also begun construction on an on-campus football stadium that was being built for $1.1 million. The chancellor

A forty-two-story building, the Cathedral of Learning on the University of Pittsburgh campus is not only the signature building at the school but also the tallest educational structure in the Western Hemisphere. It was erected about the same time that Pitt Stadium was being built. The athletic department ran well over budget on Pitt Stadium while the administration was concentrating on the Cathedral. *Courtesy of the University of Pittsburgh Athletics.*

was not necessarily a fan of the football program and became less of one after what went on with the stadium that he initially wasn't paying attention to. As it turned out, he probably should have been.

Pitt alum W.S. Hindman had designed the stadium, and the Turner Construction Company was hired to build it. The million-dollar project took thirteen months to complete and had almost doubled in cost by the time it was ready to open in 1925. It had a capacity of 69,400, almost 30,000 more than what Forbes Field offered, and it was built with the option of adding a 30,000-seat upper bowl if demand proved to be greater than anticipated. By the time it was done, the school had a more magnificent facility than it originally intended, with a price tag to match of $2.1 million.

Bowman was incensed, but the stadium was already built and the money already spent. The thought process now focused on how to get people into the stadium and make the facility pay for itself. History has taught us that the best way to get people into a stadium is to give them a winning team. Even a man like Bowman, who wasn't a fan of the program, knew that. If he thought Pitt football was out of control initially, his decision to have a more powerful program made it more so. Bowman hired Don Harrison to be his athletic director, and it became Harrison's job to figure out how to schedule big-money matchups to bring people into Pitt Stadium and help pay for the excessive overages. New coach Jock Sutherland's responsibility was to put a winning team inside the venue.

Western Pennsylvania was rich with football talent, so the trick was to figure out a way to entice these young players to stay in the area to play college ball. Harrison decided to not only offer them free tuition and books but also pay players fifty-five dollars a month, a generous amount at the time. It was a move that eventually brought pressure to Pitt from other universities, which threatened not to play the university unless it discontinued the program. Other colleges were so incensed because Pitt was more successful at these tactics than Harrison and Sutherland had hoped. Between 1925 and 1937, Pitt brought in many fans to watch the Panthers play. The school rewarded them with five national championships in twelve years.

Pitt Stadium opened on September 26, 1925, as the Panthers destroyed Washington and Lee, 26–0. It was the start of a seventy-four-year love affair (for the most part) between the historic facility and its fans. Memories of the stadium consist for the most part of the school's football program, including the five national titles with Sutherland. The team won another national championship in 1976. A Tennessee All-American by the name of

One of the greatest linemen in the history of football at the University of Pittsburgh, Rillton, Pennsylvania native Jesse Quatse was a first-team All-American in 1931. *Courtesy of the University of Pittsburgh Athletics.*

Johnny Majors performed a miracle by taking the worst football program in the nation (1-10 in 1972) and turned it into a national powerhouse four short years later with an undefeated 12-0 season. But other teams and events called this place home as well.

Located below the Gate 2 ramps in Pitt Stadium was an arena called the Pitt Pavilion, the home of the Panther basketball team. Pitt defeated Cornell in the first game played there on December 31, 1925, and called it home through the 1950–51 campaign, defeating West Virginia University (WVU) in the final contest before moving to the newly built Fitzgerald Field House in the fall. The Pavilion, with a capacity of four thousand seats, remained for forty-three years beyond its final game before being knocked down for the Duratz Athletic Complex in 1994.

Others who called Pitt Stadium home included the school's soccer and track-and-field squads; the Carnegie Tech Tartans, who played there between 1929 and 1943; the Pittsburgh Civic Light Opera (1946–58); and the Pittsburgh Steelers, who played at Pitt Stadium for one season, 1942, before making it its permanent home in 1958. The Steelers stayed there until Three Rivers Stadium was built in 1970.

After attracting many large crowds, including a record 68,918 against Fordham in 1938, the school widened the seats two inches in 1949 and discontinued the practice of allowing seating on the track area of the field, a mandate from the fire marshal. This reduced the capacity to 56,500.

The university tried to update the facility through the years, adding temporary lighting in the stadium in 1985 and making it permanent two years later, replacing the grass field with AstroTurf in 1970 and installing a video scoreboard in 1997, two years before the stadium was closed. There was a plan for an overhaul of Pitt Stadium by athletic director Ed Bozik. The $55 million upgrade would have included a roof and luxury boxes.

Unfortunately, that plan never came to fruition, and the new athletic director, Steve Pederson, decided in the mid-1990s that it would be too expensive to modernize Pitt Stadium. He decided to close it after the 1999 campaign and move to Three Rivers Stadium a year later before sharing Heinz Field with the Steelers in 2001.

The school razed the legendary stadium and, in its place, built the Petersen Events Center for the basketball program. On November 13, 1999, Pitt defeated Notre Dame, 37–27, to end the seventy-four-year run of the facility that was built so magnificently in 1925 in the shadow of the Cathedral of Learning.

15

BETTER THAN THE BEST?

Duquesne Upsets Eventual National Champion Panthers at Pitt Stadium

By Robert Healy III

I n the twenty-first century, determining the best college football team in the United States has been no easy task—not even with the Bowl Championship Series and the somehow-even-more-controversial College Football Playoff.

But most of the prior century presented an even tougher challenge to finding a true national champion. Often, nothing stood between notable schools making co-title claims than someone with a poll, a survey or some sort of formula. Indeed, multiple schools claim national championships in the same major college football season.

Duquesne University, for example, claims an undefeated 1941 season as a national-title campaign, but the universities of Alabama and Minnesota also say 1941 was theirs. And with no NCAA trophy ever handed out for the highest level of college football, who's to say any of those teams was worse than the other was? None of those teams played each other that season, after all. But at least Minnesota was also undefeated.

A similarly confusing situation arose in 1936, with Minnesota and the University of Pittsburgh, both one-loss teams, staking legitimate claims to national titles.

Minnesota lost, 6–0, on the road to Northwestern University for the Golden Gophers' only blemish that season. Pitt and Fordham University played to a scoreless tie at the Polo Grounds. But the only loss for the

Mike Basrak was Duquesne football's first All-American and was a key member of the Dukes football team that defeated Pitt before beating Mississippi State in the 1937 Orange Bowl. Basrak was named the MVP of the Orange Bowl that season. *Courtesy of Duquesne University Athletics.*

Panthers came two weeks earlier, a 7–0 upset by crosstown Duquesne at Pitt Stadium on October 17.

The win took the Dukes to 4-0 on the season and an appearance in the AP's inaugural weekly national poll. But Duquesne disappointingly lost its next two games, 2–0 to West Virginia Wesleyan College and 14–7 on the road to the University of Detroit, before going 4-0 down the stretch, including a 13–12 win over Mississippi State in the January 1, 1937, Orange Bowl.

Despite the major-bowl win and seven shutouts, no selectors of note declared the Dukes national champs for 1936, their strength of schedule a likely contributor to that.

The loss to Duquesne could have been devastating to the Panthers' season, but they shut out their next two opponents, the AP's no. 7 University of Notre Dame and the aforementioned Fordham Rams, who were ranked fifth, to get back on track.

Pitt's defense was outstanding during the 1936 season, shutting out six opponents, and its offense could light up the scoreboard. The Panthers put up a 93–0 combined score in the three games before the tilt with the Dukes, including an 87–0 count at Pitt Stadium.

The Panthers program was among the best in the country, especially in the east, in this era. Pitt also claims national titles for the 1915, 1916, 1918, 1929, 1931 and 1934 seasons (and 1937, for that matter).

The Dukes hadn't even scored a point on a Pitt football team until the second quarter of the 1936 game, when substitute halfback George Matsik found a hole on the left side and raced 71 yards over wet turf for the game's only touchdown. Boyd Brumbaugh added the extra point.

"For an instant he [Matsik] seems to be trapped by two Panther linemen," *Pittsburgh Press* sports editor Chester Smith wrote in a front-page recap the following day, "but somehow he wriggles into the open and now, by a frantic twist of his body and a pivot which is perfectly done, he has gone."

A headline in that day's issue of the *Press* called Matsik's run against the "Great Pitt Eleven" a "Shot Heard 'Round the World." To Smith, the Dukes showed themselves to be the better team, at least for a day.

"At the finish there is no thought that the better team did not win," Smith wrote, "for Duquesne had the better of this…even though she can add up but three first downs to Pitt's 11. The Hilltoppers [another Duquesne nickname] gained 209 yards to the Panthers' 200 and the score is as it should have been."

Special police presence was required after the game at area hotels and theaters to quell Dukes fans, according to the *Press*. Police also fended off Duquesne revelers trying to take the Pitt Stadium goalposts "amid shouts of, 'The cops are defending the goal better than Pitt did!'"

Pitt would more than rebound, winning the Rose Bowl, 21–0, over AP no. 5 University of Washington on New Year's Day 1937.

16

THE DAY THE ON-CAMPUS, OFF-CAMPUS DEBATE BEGAN

The Pitt Stadium Finale

By David Finoli

As I was perusing Facebook one day, I saw on one of the fan groups yet another "Should Pitt build an on-campus football stadium?" debate. The debates appear often and are usually filled with emotion on both sides. Reading them generally takes me back to a special date in Pitt football history, November 13, 1999. The Panthers hosted Notre Dame in the final contest held in historic Pitt Stadium. On that day, seventy-four years of history came to an end. In the stadium's place would be student housing and a state-of-the-art basketball arena. It was also the day this debate commenced. When Pitt moved to Three Rivers Stadium for the 2000 season, fans and alumni alike began arguing this point.

After the university unceremoniously fired coach Mike Gottfried before its successful 1989 season ended, Pitt began one of the worst eras in the program's history. Walt Harris had seemingly stabilized the program when he was hired in 1997, but they finished 2-9 a year later and stood at only 4-5 before the Notre Dame game. It would not be acceptable to lose to one of the school's fiercest rivals in the final game at a storied stadium that saw six national championships captured within its walls.

The program was definitely in disrepair, and little was printed in the paper about this important day. Only a few miscellaneous stories appeared. One reported on a retired Pitt Stadium worker who hoped to find a wedding

Opened in 1925, Pitt Stadium was considered one of the preeminent college stadiums of the time. It originally had a capacity of 69,400 fans. In the first twelve seasons it was opened, the Panthers captured five national championships. *Courtesy of the University of Pittsburgh Athletics.*

ring he had lost in the stadium thirty years before. My guess is that ring went down with the bricks.

Free safety D.J. Dinkins, a senior, gave an impassioned speech prior to the game before a sold-out crowd of 60,190, including some of the greatest Pitt players ever to take the field: Tony Dorsett, Joe Schmidt, Marshall Goldberg, Bill Fralic and Roger Kingdom. The speech fired up the Panthers, who played one of the most inspired games the program experienced since Gottfried was fired ten years earlier.

The game was an incredible battle from the outset. Every time Pitt vaulted ahead, the Fighting Irish battled back. The score was tied, 10–10, at the half, then again at 17–17 in the third quarter before the Panthers vaulted ahead, 20–17. Redshirt freshman free safety Ramon Walker, who was having a great contest, forced a fumble and returned it deep into Notre Dame territory. John Turman hit Antonio Bryant from 28 yards out to give the home team a 10-point lead. Notre Dame quickly answered with a touchdown of their own before the two teams traded field goals, making the score 30-27 as the exciting contest neared its end.

Notre Dame had the ball with a chance to take the lead, but the Panthers were destined to win this contest. A pass came toward the middle. Walker nailed the receiver, forcing the ball to pop up. Freshman linebacker Scott McCurley, who had blocked a 36-yard field goal attempt earlier in the game, picked off the pass and returned it to the Irish 44. Not wanting a costly turnover, Pitt decided to run the ball, handing off nine out of ten plays. The Irish defensive line was tiring, and Pitt's offensive line was now dominating them. Finally, Kevan Barlow bolted in from 8 yards out to put the game out of reach, 37–27, with only 1:41 remaining.

The visitors drove to the Panther 13 but turned the ball over with nine seconds left. Pitt never got a chance to finish the game, as the fans stormed the field and pulled down the goal posts to celebrate this historic ending. Officials decided to end the game at that point, and the Panthers walked off with one of the greatest victories in Pitt Stadium's seventy-four-year run. It also began this damned argument that apparently will never end. Personally, I'm OK watching the games from my seats at Heinz Field. Oakland never had the infrastructure or parking to make going to a game at an on-campus facility an easy experience, but I have to admit that I miss walking up Cardiac Hill to watch the Panthers. I guess I can see both sides.

17

THERE USED TO BE A
BASKETBALL ARENA HERE

The Pitt Pavilion Is Built Underneath Pitt Stadium

By David Finoli

Y ou'd think the odds would be stacked very much in favor of the fact that Pitt Stadium was nothing more than a football facility. If you bet that way, you'd come up a loser. It wasn't just a football stadium, and the soccer and track-and-field squads weren't the only other University of Pittsburgh tenants to play there. Of all things, the basketball program called it home for twenty-six years. The team didn't play games on a court in the middle of a football field, which is a current trend for the March Madness Final Four. One of the little-known facts about Pitt Stadium is that a basketball arena was built underneath the ramp at Gate 2. On December 31, 1925, a couple of months after the football squad christened the new stadium, Pitt basketball took on Cornell in the initial contest at the new facility, the Pitt Pavilion.

While many celebrated the state-of-the-art football facility, few ever gave the same kudos to the basketball arena. There was room for four thousand fans on wooden stands, and there was only one entrance into the arena, which caused issues on big game evenings. The place was dirty, damp and cold. The visitors had to change in a locker room meant for football, then go outside in the cold winter air, walk down a dirty and sometimes muddy path and wipe off their shoes before walking on to the court. The venue was dubbed the "Ice Box" and was so cold that players used to keep their warmups on until the beginning of the game and fans rarely took off their coats.

Arguably the greatest basketball coach the University of Pittsburgh has ever known, Henry Clifford "Doc" Carlson led the school to its only two national championships (1928 and 1930), as well as its lone Final Four appearance (1941). Finishing his thirty-one-year career at Pitt with a 367-248 mark, Carlson was inducted into the Naismith Basketball Hall of Fame in 1959. *Courtesy of the University of Pittsburgh Athletics.*

A 2002 *Pittsburgh Post-Gazette* article by Gerry Dulac quoted Pitt legend Lou "Bimbo" Cecconi: "To me it was absolutely the worst, but it was Pitt Stadium and I accepted it. I didn't realize how bad it was until later. It was nothing but a hole in the wall." The same article quoted Bernie Artman, a guard on the 1951 squad. That season, the Panthers moved out of the

Pavilion and into the Fitzgerald Field House. Artman said that it was "the worst facility you could imagine. The first time I saw it I said I didn't want to go to Pitt."

As bad as the facility was—and from all accounts it was pretty bad—the Panthers played some of the best basketball in the program's history there, winning their only two national championships at their "hole in the wall."

Even though most people had the same thoughts as Cecconi and Artman, when it opened on New Year's Eve 1925, fans and media alike had a different view.

Over 1,800 fans came to the Pavilion on December 31, with the Panthers underdogs against a powerful Cornell University squad. It had been some time since Pitt basketball drew that large a crowd. After the favorites started out with a 7–3 lead, the Panthers dominated the rest of the contest in an impressive 36–26 victory.

In a preview of the contest in the *Pittsburgh Press* on New Year's Eve, the paper exclaimed that the Pitt Pavilion was "one of the most remarkable basketball auditoriums in the country. The lighting system is perfection itself, and the course of the ball, as it passes from one speedster to another, or is dribbled down the floor, can be seen without any difficulty." The description was in stark contrast to the feelings of players and fans alike when the venue closed over twenty-five years later. Then again, heat and comfort may not have been important in 1925.

When the Panthers defeated their rivals, the West Virginia Mountaineers, on February 26, 1951, 74–72, the papers exclaimed that the "Ice Box Era" was coming to an end. As in the opening contest, Pitt was an underdog on this evening, scoring the final 8 points for the win.

And just like, that the Pitt Pavilion was closed. While this venue may have been the worst facility a major Pittsburgh team ever played in, a sports arena is also remembered for the memories it invoked. It was on this dank court that the Panthers were at their best, winning the national championship in 1928 and 1930 and going to the school's only Final Four in 1941. Cold or not, no other Pitt basketball facility came close to turning out those kinds of memories.

18

THE FRUITLESS VENTURE FINALLY ENDS

Pitt Scores against Fordham

By David Finoli

For three years, two of the nation's most powerful football teams faced off against each other in the famed Polo Grounds in New York: the University of Pittsburgh Panthers and the Fordham University Rams. Between 1935 and 1937, their battles resulted in no points. That's right, three consecutive 0–0 ties. In 1937, Pitt thought they finally broke the fruitless venture with a score, but Marshall Goldberg's touchdown on a reverse was called back on a holding call by lineman Tony Matisi. With the touchdown taken off the board, the game ended with another 0–0 tie. Multiple turnovers cost the two schools scoring opportunities, as did missed field goal attempts. In a book I wrote with Chris Fletcher, *Steel City Gridirons*, I compared the three contests to Sisyphus, the man who kept pushing a boulder up a hill only to have it roll back down. This was the Pitt-Fordham rivalry for these three years. When the teams finally left the New York City boundary for Pitt Stadium in 1938, the three-year fruitless streak finally came to an end, as the Panthers broke through the scoreless shackles in a big way.

The Panthers came into this matchup on the heels of back-to-back national championships in 1936 and 1937 and were looking for a third, possessing a 5-0 mark and outscoring their opponents 134–19. While it was the greatest era in the history of the program under coach John "Jock" Sutherland, it was shifting into a more difficult time despite the national titles.

At the 1937 Rose Bowl, where Pitt won its first bowl game with a 21–0 thrashing of Washington, Sutherland and his players were upset because

The greatest football coach to ever roam the sidelines at the University of Pittsburgh, Jock Sutherland (*far left*) talks to his star running back Marshall Goldberg (*far right*). Goldberg finished third in the Heisman Trophy voting in 1937 and second in 1938. *Courtesy of the University of Pittsburgh Athletics.*

the Huskies had sported new suits and were given $100 each in expense money. According to Goldberg in a 1987 *Los Angeles Times* article by Gordon Edes: "Those fellows (Washington) came in with new suits and new watches, and had $100 each in expense money. We got a gold football and a blanket. Jock was more upset than anyone else." Because of the controversy, the irritated Pitt players voted to not go to a bowl game the following season despite an undefeated year. Chancellor John Bowman, who wasn't a fan of the program to begin with, was upset at the decision and eventually began the process of de-emphasis, which eliminated athletic scholarships and stipends. This led to the resignation of Sutherland at the end of the 1938 campaign and the end of Pitt as a consistent national power until the mid-1970s. Despite the ensuing controversy, at this point, the Panthers were the best team in the land. And despite being outplayed for three quarters of this contest, Pitt would have one of its greatest victories under their Hall-of-Fame coach—and, as it turned out, their last big victory under him.

Pitt finally broke the three-year scoreless drought early on when Bill Daddio hit on a first-quarter 12-yard field goal in front of a record crowd of 75,587 at Pitt Stadium. But Fordham would score the first touchdown by either team in more than three games to vault ahead, 7–3, a lead they would hold until Pitt finally took control of the contest in the final quarter.

Pitt had one of the country's great backfields in 1938, which was referred to as the "Dream Backfield," and they ran over the Rams. Dick Cassiano scored once, and Goldberg accounted for two touchdowns in what turned out to be an impressive 24–13 victory. The scoreless nightmare was over, and the Panthers were considered the top team in the nation at that point. Unfortunately, this impressive victory proved to be the end of the greatest era in the program's history. They were upset by Carnegie Tech, 20–10, before losing to Duke in the season finale to finish 8-2. Sutherland resigned at the end of the season, and the program soon fell on hard times with its new restrictive football policy. On this day, though, they accomplished what no Pitt or Fordham team had done in four years: score points.

19

A PICTURE FOR THE AGES

A Bloodied Y.A. Tittle Kneels on the Turf at Pitt Stadium

By David Finoli

By 1964, the New York Giants had a reputation for being one of the best franchises in the history of the NFL. The Pittsburgh Steelers, on the other hand, had a reputation of a loser. The Giants were coming off an East Division championship, and their thirty-seven-year-old quarterback, Hall of Famer Y.A. Tittle, was the Associated Press NFL Most Valuable Player. Pittsburgh had been a winning team in 1963 with a 7-4-3 mark but would return to its losing ways a year later. For New York, 1963 proved to be the end of their championship run, as their stars were showing their age. After a humiliating 38–7 loss to the Philadelphia Eagles in the season opener, the Giants traveled to Pitt Stadium to play the Steelers. New York ended up dropping the 27–24 contest to Pittsburgh that afternoon. But the loss would eventually be forgotten. What lives on about that September 20, 1964 game was a photograph of Tittle, his knees on the ground, his helmet off and blood streaming down his face. It's a picture that has lived on through the years and is considered one of the greatest sports photographs ever taken.

The game began like many Giant-Steeler games had in the era, with New York breaking out to a big lead, 14–0, as the first half was coming to an end. Then the play happened. Linebacker John Baker broke in and crushed the legendary quarterback. The ball floated into rookie defensive tackle Chuck Hinton's hands, and he strolled in from 8 yards out to make the score 13–6 after Mike Clark's extra point was blocked.

After a seventy-four-year run, Pitt Stadium ended its tenure on November 13, 1999, when the Panthers defeated Notre Dame, 37–27, in front of 60,190 fans. *Courtesy of the University of Pittsburgh Athletics.*

As the play finished, Tittle was on the ground. The newspaper photographer for the *Pittsburgh Post-Gazette*, Morris Berman, was working the game and snapped a picture of the play and of the fallen Hall of Famer.

At the time, Berman was more famous as a photographer during World War II, known for his pictures of Italian dictator Benito Mussolini and his mistress, Clara Petacci, after they had been killed and hung by their heels as the war came to an end. He had snapped several pictures during the game, including the iconic one of Tittle. Berman was trying to convince his photo editor to print that picture, but the editor felt that, since there was no action in it, it shouldn't be included in the sports section the next day. A look at the sports section of the paper for September 21, you'll see that the famed photo does not appear—a grave miscalculation.

Berman had a great eye for photography and knew he had shot an exceptional photograph of Tittle, so he entered it in contests and won the National Headliner award for sports photograph of the year in 1964. The former photograph director of *National Geographic*, Rich Clarkson, said in the obituary of Berman in the *Los Angeles Times*, written by Jon Thurber on June 21, 2002: "It said a lot to people that sometimes the most revealing sports photograph was made after the play was done or the game was over. It capitalized on the value of its emotion. It led other photographers to open their eyes to things other than peak action."

The photo ended up taking on a life of its own and was included in an HBO documentary celebrating the best sports photography of the twentieth century, *Picture Perfect: The Stories Behind the Greatest Photographs in Sports*. It was a shot that Tittle himself never liked, one he referred to as the "Blood Picture."

As for the game itself, it was an exciting contest. The Steelers won without the injured Hall-of-Fame quarterback under center for the opponent. Tittle had cracked his sternum and suffered a concussion on the play, 27–24.

The game at Pitt Stadium has been long forgotten, but the scene of Y.A. Tittle on the ground will always be remembered as one of the most iconic moments to happen inside its walls.

20

PIE IN THE SKY

Pitt's Tony Dorsett Helps Bring the Program from the Basement to a National Championship by Slicing Up an Old Rival

By Chris Fletcher

Rhubarb pie changed the fortunes of the University of Pittsburgh's football program. It wasn't the all-American apple pie or the tremendously overrated pumpkin pie that we're forced to endure each fall. It was rhubarb pie: a glorious mix of diced rhubarb stalk (the leaves are poisonous), some sliced strawberries, a little flour, a lot of sugar and a spoonful of grated lemon peel, slipped between two flakey crusts.

Rhubarb pie was newly hired coach Johnny Majors's secret weapon in luring one Anthony Drew Dorsett to sign at Pitt. Majors knew that if he was going to turn around a program after a 1-10 season, he was going to have to attract the best players from the area. And Dorsett was *the* prized recruit.

Though small at five feet, eleven inches and weighing all of 157 pounds, Dorsett had a long list of suitors. In fact, representatives from sixty-eight schools reached out, hoping to secure the services of the All-American from Hopewell High. His speed and elusiveness marked him as a game-changing talent, the kind that can turn a woeful program around. Majors had an advantage, and he pressed it. Dorsett was local.

Ten times Majors made the trek from Oakland to Dorsett's home in Aliquippa, often accompanied by treats and soft drinks. On the clinching visit, he came bearing rhubarb pie, made from an old family recipe from Pitt assistant coach Jackie Sherril's seventy-year-old mother in the heart of pie country, Biloxi, Mississippi.

Tony Dorsett (*number 33 in dark jersey*) breaks out on a long run. Dorsett's historic career at Pitt would end with him being the first running back to break the 2,000-yard barrier in a season and over 6,000 yards in a career. *Courtesy of the University of Pittsburgh Athletics.*

One program that didn't covet Dorsett was Notre Dame. Coach Ara Parseghian thought Dorsett was too small. Actually, the rumor was that the coach's exact words were, "The skinny, little kid from Aliquippa never would make it as a major college running back." That would come back to haunt the Irish and serve as motivation for Dorsett. In addition to the chance to play in front of his family and friends, the chance for sweet revenge on Notre Dame pushed Dorsett to "bulk up" to 170 pounds without losing any of his trademark speed. Every year, he circled the Notre Dame game on the schedule.

In their first seasons at Pitt, both Majors and his running back had an impact. Heading into a November showdown with Notre Dame, Pitt sported a 5-2-1 record. Much of that success came from Dorsett. In only eight games, he had already topped 1,100 yards rushing. The Irish presented the biggest challenge of the season, coming in with the nation's top-ranked rushing defense.

That didn't matter to Dorsett. On a cold, snowy day at Pitt Stadium, Dorsett carried the ball 29 times for 209 yards, including a 65-yard romp. Despite outgaining a superior opponent and Dorsett's heroics, Pitt fell, 31–

10. His efforts drew praise from coach Parseghian, who said, "He's definitely someone to watch."

The next year in South Bend, Dorsett was hobbled after spraining an ankle the week before against Temple. It also didn't help that Notre Dame Stadium was a mess. Snow and rain made the footing bad, and with a heavily taped ankle, Dorsett rushed for only 61 yards, one of the lowest totals of his college career. This time, Pitt came close, with Notre Dame holding on to a hard-fought 14–10 win.

With the series traveling back to Pitt Stadium the next year, Dorsett would be a on a fast track for a record-setting performance. On Pitt's first possession, Dorsett zipped for 14 yards. A few plays later, he was gone, blasting through the left side of the Irish line for 57 yards. On Pitt's next possession, he dashed 71 yards for a TD. His stat line at that point: 4 carries for a gaudy 151 yards. For good measure, he closed out the half with a 49-yard touchdown reception. Pitt won, 34–20.

No one had ever run roughshod over Notre Dame like that before. No back had ever piled up that kind of yardage—303 yards on the ground on 23 carries, as well as 71 yards in receptions. That's nearly the length of four football fields.

In his final game against Notre Dame, the South Bend grounds crew tried to help slow down Dorsett by letting the grass grow. It didn't matter. Dorsett finished with 181 rushing yards and completed a feast against Irish defenders in a 31–10 victory.

Pitt went from 1-10 and the basement of the East to a national championship in just four years. The games against Notre Dame served as a testament to his and the team's ascendancy. In four games against Notre Dame from 1973 to 1976 (two victories, two defeats), Dorsett ran for 754 yards on 96 attempts, which stands as a college football record for a player against one team. For Dorsett, it was easy as pie.

21

STEELERS SAY SAYONARA TO OAKLAND AFTER 1969 SEASON

By Tom Rooney

From their inaugural 1933 season, when Pittsburgh's NFL's expansion team was first called the Pirates, until the end of the 1969 campaign, the Steelers (the name was changed in 1940) played their home games in Oakland, first at Forbes Field and then at Pitt Stadium. The team actually alternated games in both venues during the season for several years. Gate attractions like the "Turnpike Rival" Cleveland Browns would warrant the larger Oakland Oval on Cardiac Hill before Pitt Stadium was eventually scheduled for all Steeler home games.

Like those baseball Pirates, that 1970 Steeler squad headed to the North Shore and the state-of-the-art Three Rivers Stadium. It was déjà vu for the baseball Bucs, who had departed the North Side and Exposition Park in 1909, when the ultramodern Forbes Field opened its gates.

Joe Gordon knew Oakland, and he knew sports. A star at Taylor Allderdice High in the bordering neighborhood of Squirrel Hill, he was an infielder with Pitt's baseball team. Gordon first worked at a few nonsport trades, including selling Yellow Pages ads and furnishings for Roth Rugs. But when he took a sales position in the red- hot aluminum siding market, it came with a caveat. He would also become a player for Mario Noce's company softball team. An evening game in a community was preceded by a full-court press on siding sales earlier in the day.

Gordon then traversed over the "Hill" from Oakland to jobs at the new Civic Arena. After stints with the Pittsburgh Rens of the American

Basketball League, which folded on New Year's Eve in the middle of the second, 1962–63, season, Gordon moved on to the minor league hockey Pittsburgh Hornets and then stayed in the same PR job with the 1967 NHL expansion Penguins. Two years later, the Steelers were expanding their department, and Gordon became the team's director of publicity just ahead of the 1969 training camp in Latrobe, Pennsylvania.

"Latrobe, dorm rooms with no air conditioning in the middle of steaming summers, way out in the country, that was a big change for me for a city guy like me," Gordon recalled.

Gordon's first office location working for the Steelers was at their Roosevelt Hotel headquarters in downtown Pittsburgh in that summer of '69, just four months after the team hired Chuck Noll as its new head coach. Also new to the team was first-round draft pick Joe Greene, who would anchor a defense that helped produce four Super Bowl championships in six years, earn the team the unofficial designation of "Team of the 1970s" and establish a modern-day dynasty.

That Pitt Stadium swan song season of 1969 saw the Steelers win on September 21, opening day, at home against the Detroit Lions, 16–13. It was the last home opener in Oakland. Another rookie, Warren Bankston, ran for a late touchdown, and the defense held. There was jubilation for new coach Noll, but it was short-lived. The Steelers lost the last thirteen straight, including an all-too-familiar heartbreaker against the New York Giants, 21–17, at Pitt Stadium on December 14—the Steelers' last game in Oakland. The Black and Gold led late, but the Giants' punter pulled a fake and ran for a late first down, and Hall-of-Fame Quarterback Fran Tarkenton threw his third touchdown. That indirectly led to another Hall-of-Fame quarterback coming to Pittsburgh via the first pick of the 1970 draft: Terry Bradshaw. Press pictures of the time show the fresh-faced Bradshaw with a full head of hair in Three Rivers Stadium while it was still under construction.

Steelers founder and primary owner Art Rooney hated to lose, and he chafed at criticism that he wasn't really trying. Gordon had seen earlier how dearly Rooney wanted to win after four decades of football failings and follies. "We were in Green Bay for a preseason game and the Steelers had a lead late but the center hiked the ball over Quarterback Dick Shiner's head and the Packers won in the last minute," Gordon recalled. "Art took the cigar out of his mouth and tossed it forward in frustration. It hit the press box window in front of him and bounced back on his lap."

The two Joes, Gordon and Greene, established a special bond that went well beyond the typical PR guy–team star relationship. Years into their tremendous success, Gordon was allowed to address the team about some of the players' desire to reduce access to the press. The Steelers players were starting to feel suffocated from the daily local and national coverage that comes with being successful in a sport that was experiencing exponential growth.

"I explained to the team that we, the Steelers, were known for having the best media access in the league and as its biggest attraction, we needed to maintain that, and we had a responsibility to the league," Gordon remembered. He left the locker room so the players could talk. The next day, he ran into Greene and inquired, "Well, what about the issue with access the players complained about?"

Greene smiled and asked in turn, "And exactly what issue would that have been?"

Unlike the collegiate Pitt Panthers, the NFL Pittsburgh teams never won a title in Oakland, either at Forbes Field or at Pitt Stadium. So it was not a sad sayonara to a lot of even sadder Steeler Sundays.

22

WE'RE NO. 1

Pitt Beats Army and Ascends to No. 1 in the Polls

By David Finoli

There are many memories of the University of Pittsburgh Panthers' 1976 national championship season: Tony Dorsett and crew defeating Notre Dame on the road before a national television audience in the opener; Dorsett breaking the NCAA career rushing mark against Navy; Pitt finally defeating Penn State for the first time under Joe Paterno; and the Panthers winning the title against Georgia in the Sugar Bowl. The one thing those four moments had in common was that none of them happened on the Pitt Stadium turf. The most memorable moment there occurred on November 6, as Pitt took on Army. The thing about this wonderful moment was that it wasn't about anything happening in the second-ranked Panthers' 37–7 destruction of the Cadets. Rather, it concerned a contest taking place 436 miles away in West Lafayette, Indiana, as Purdue was taking on top-ranked Michigan at Ross-Ade Stadium. It was the day Purdue upset the Wolverines, 16–14. Fans at Pitt Stadium celebrated the fact that the Panthers would now ascend to the no. 1 spot that Michigan had just vacated.

I was a sophomore at Greensburg Central Catholic at the time, and my friends and I were at the school for the Sadie Hawkins Dance. Today, a Sadie Hawkins Dance means you have a date, it's in the evening and you're going to have to ante up decent money for a suit. Back then, it was a group of students on a Saturday afternoon in jeans and T-shirts. While others were dancing and socializing, I was in the corner with

Pictured here is the land where Pitt Stadium used to sit. The view is from the Petersen Events Center, the current home of basketball at the University of Pittsburgh. It replaced Pitt Stadium after it closed in 1999. *Courtesy of David Finoli.*

my radio, listening to the Pitt game while waiting for Purdue-Michigan updates.

I can't say this was the most popular thing to do at a dance, but as the game went on, more and more of my friends gathered by my radio in hopes of hearing the news that was coming out of West Lafayette. As far as the contest at Pitt Stadium went, Carson Long kicked three field goals, and Dorsett scored three touchdowns on his way to 212 yards as Matt Cavanaugh finally returned to the field after a month on the sidelines with a fractured ankle. But none of that seemed to matter to us or the 45,573 fans at the stadium. As the day went on, Purdue was holding its own against the heavily favored Wolverines.

After pulling ahead, 7–0, in the first quarter, Michigan gave up two Boilermaker touchdowns by Scott Dierking to fall behind, 13–7, at the half. Quarterback Rick Leach then put the top-ranked Wolverines up, 14–13, with a 65-yard touchdown pass to future Steeler Jim Smith in the third quarter. Pitt fans in western Pennsylvania and beyond were holding their collective breath as Michigan was driving in the fourth quarter to put the game away. Then it happened. With twelve minutes left, the Wolverines' great running back Rob Lytle fumbled the ball at the Purdue 29. They drove down the field, only to be stopped at the Wolverine 11. Purdue kicker Rick Supan nailed a 23-yard field goal to put the underdogs up, 16–14. When the score was announced at the stadium, the place went nuts.

Michigan wasn't going to give up without a fight. They went on a drive themselves, taking it to the Boilermaker 19 as time was running out. This wasn't the era of multimedia, so we didn't have the broadcast of the game, only the updates being brought by the Pitt Stadium announcer, which were then translated to us by Pitt announcer Bill Hillgrove.

Finally, Wolverine kicker Bob Wood lined up for the game-winning field goal. The tension was incredible. Since Pitt couldn't face off against Michigan that year—they would head to a Rose Bowl matchup against the Pac 10 champion—this might have been the only chance they had to vault over the Wolverines to no. 1. Finally, after moments of torturous silence, the fans at the stadium heard the words they wanted so desperately to hear when Wood missed the kick. The PA announcer blurted out, "We're no. 1!" To borrow a quote from legendary announcer Chuck Thomson when he called Bill Mazeroski's legendary home run, "Pittsburgh is now an insane asylum."

The Sadie Hawkins Dance at Greensburg Central Catholic was also an insane asylum. We were screaming at the fact that Wood missed the field goal. Pitt would now be no. 1 and have their destiny in their own hands with three games left in the season. It was the greatest moment at Pitt Stadium that season, a result of a score in a game occurring four hundred miles away.

23

THE TRACK JOHN WOODRUFF CALLED HOME

By David Finoli

While most of the history of Pitt Stadium deals with the Panther football program, there were people in other sports who called the stadium home. In soccer, Joe Luxbacher was one of the greatest players to ever wear the Blue and Gold for Pitt. He played there between 1970 and 1973 before becoming the team's coach in 1984. He remained in that position until he retired in 2015. The track team also ran at Pitt Stadium and produced many tremendous male and female athletes over the years. Perhaps none was more renowned than the man who was able to turn his nose up at Hitler in the 1936 Berlin Olympics with a dramatic gold-medal performance in the 800-meter run. That man was John Woodruff.

Born in Connellsville, Pennsylvania, about fifty miles outside of Pittsburgh, Woodruff, who passed away in 2007 at the age of ninety-two, is still a legend in his hometown. There is a section of a wall in a popular Connellsville restaurant, Bud Murphy's, dedicated to Woodruff's magnificent achievements, including his feat in Berlin.

Hitler was unhappy that so many African American athletes were on the U.S.A. track team and was even more incensed that they were having success. Jesse Owens was the most famous of these athletes, capturing four gold medals and helping to dismantle Hitler's dream of Aryan supremacy. But Woodruff achieved his fame in a most exciting manner. As the 800-meter final began, the Pitt freshman got stuck among the runners in what was a slow pace. Not gaining any ground, he decided to employ a controversial

As a freshman at the University of Pittsburgh in 1936, John Woodruff qualified for the 800-meter race at the Berlin Olympics. In the race, Woodruff made a stunning move to get out of traffic and came from behind to win the gold medal. His career also included a share of the 4-by-880 world relay record with the national team and an Amateur Athletic Union title in the 800 in 1937. *Courtesy of the University of Pittsburgh Athletics.*

strategy that rarely succeeded. Woodruff slowed down, almost stopping, to allow the runners to get around him. This put him in open space. He felt that this was his only chance to win. He got into an open lane and, remarkably, sped past the field. His strides were incredibly long as he vaulted toward the front. He sprinted down the stretch, finally getting past Italy's Mario Lanzi and holding on for the gold medal. It was his crowning achievement, and he went on to have arguably the greatest career of any Pitt track athlete.

The Connellsville native was undefeated at Pitt Stadium, losing his only collegiate race his freshman year at West Virginia. Woodruff is the only men's track athlete from the University of Pittsburgh to win three NCAA championships, which he did between 1937 and 1939.

He wasn't always welcomed at Pitt with open arms. John desperately wanted to be a football player while at Connellsville High School, but he left school to help his family financially during the Depression by getting a job at a local glass factory. The plant wasn't interested in hiring a Black man, so he went back to school, where he eventually joined the track team. Woodruff started out in the shot put before finding a home running the half mile, for which he set state records and secured a scholarship at Pitt. He was one of only twelve African Americans at the school and ended up staying at the YMCA in the Hill District and secured a job cleaning at Pitt Stadium as well as the Pitt Pavilion.

In his freshman year, John finished second at the AAUs in the 800, qualifying him for the 1936 U.S. Olympic track team before his march to history later that summer. While the university wasn't always an open place for him, after he concluded his time at Pitt, he eventually became one of the school's greatest ambassadors. Following his death, chancellor Mark Nordenberg said: "John Woodruff's story was a remarkable one. The people in our University and community loved John Woodruff. We stood in awe of his athletic achievements, but we also admired him as a human being who helped advance humanity's cause through the values he held and promoted. His lifetime and lifeline of achievements placed him and Pitt in the embrace of the vast and the eternal."

It was the perfect way to describe the man who just might have been the greatest athlete to perform on the Pitt Stadium stage.

24

REVENGE IS SWEET

The Pitt-USC Rivalry in the Sutherland Era

By David Finoli

Even though the early days of the Pitt-USC rivalry occurred in the Panthers' most celebrated era, the Trojans were the one team that coach Jock Sutherland and his squad could not get past. The first two times they met were as a reward for an outstanding season, with a trip to Pasadena to play in the Rose Bowl. Both times, the Panthers went in fully believing they'd walk away with a signature victory; both times, they were sent home after being crushed by a combined 82–14 for the two contests. One had to wonder why Sutherland invited this dominant USC team to Pitt Stadium in 1934. Losing in California was one thing, but the potential of getting humiliated on their home turf was another. As it turned out, when the game clock struck zero, the fans were happy, feeling just how sweet revenge can be.

Howard Jones, the Hall-of-Fame coach of Southern California, had been the lone coach in the country to figure out how to dominate Sutherland's powerful Panthers. He had won four national titles in his time at USC, and there was little reason to believe that just because he brought his team east the result would be any different—except for the fact that red flags were showing up that the Trojans might be in trouble.

After three dominant wins to begin the season, USC was upset by Washington State, 19–0, before traveling to the Steel City. There were reports that the team had gone "Hollywood" and wasn't putting in the effort it had in the past that made them such an incredible program.

Four members of the Pitt football team having fun in preparation for the 1937 Rose Bowl. Pictured second from left is college football Hall of Famer Ave Daniell. *Courtesy of the University of Pittsburgh Athletics.*

In the book *Classic 'Burgh: The 50 Greatest Collegiate Games in Pittsburgh Sports History*, the USC school paper, the *Daily Trojan*, is quoted: "The team had little to say on the charges they were largely a group of Hollywood-struck boys who were as toys in the clutches of film queens and movie magnets." Jones was sick of the rumors and set out to push his team in preparation for this contest. He figured he knew how to beat the Panthers but wanted to make sure his club was focused on the task at hand.

Over 55,000 fans showed up at Pitt Stadium on October 13, 1934, to see if Pitt could break the stranglehold USC had over them and hoping the rumors coming out of Los Angeles were true. We can't say for sure that the Trojan players were just boy toys for Hollywood starlets, but we do know that, from the outset, they didn't appear ready to play.

USCs Bill Howard fumbled on the first possession of the game, and Pitt's Mike Nicksic pounced on it. After a 9-yard run by Nicksic, Izzy Weinstock did something for the Panthers that had never happened in the history of the rivalry to that point: he scored a touchdown that gave Pitt a lead over the

Trojans. In the second quarter, Heinie Weisenbaugh ran for 31 yards before a 2-yard scamper that remarkably put Pitt up, 13–0. USC finally woke up with a touchdown of their own on an 8-yard run by Calvin Clemens, and the two teams went into the locker room with the Panther lead cut to 13–7.

No one knew what would happen in the second half. Could Pitt hold on to the lead? Would the Trojans finally wake up and dominate the Panthers as they had in the past? After a poor 11-yard USC punt that gave the Panthers the ball inside Trojan territory, the fans had their answer. Verne Baxter pulled in a 49-yard pass for a touchdown to give Pitt the cushion they needed in a 20–6 win.

In the end, it didn't matter how bad the Panthers had been beaten in their two Rose Bowl appearances against USC, and it didn't matter if the Trojans were focused more on starlets than playbooks. Pitt had the victory it wanted so badly. And it found out exactly how sweet revenge is.

25

THE GREATEST COACH EVER TO ROAM THE SIDELINES AT PITT STADIUM

Jock Sutherland

By David Finoli

When it comes to the debate about the greatest coach to roam the sidelines at Pitt Stadium, the answer really begins and ends with the first coach to have the honor: John "Jock" Sutherland. In this chapter, we not only look to answer that easiest of questions, but we also consider where Sutherland stands in terms of all football coaches in Western Pennsylvania history and all managers and coaches to lead teams in this area.

Greatest Coaches at Pitt Stadium

1. Jock Sutherland
2. Jackie Sherrill
3. Johnny Majors
4. John Michelosen
5. Buddy Parker

This subject would be a little more dramatic if we could include Pop Warner and Chuck Noll, but Warner never had the opportunity to coach at Pitt Stadium, and the lone year Noll coached on its turf he was anything

Arguably the greatest football coach the city has ever seen, John "Jock" Sutherland compiled a career record of 111-20-12 while leading the Panthers to five national championships in fifteen seasons at the helm of the program. He also led the Pittsburgh Steelers to their first postseason contest, in 1947. *Courtesy of the University of Pittsburgh Athletics.*

but great, losing thirteen consecutive games after winning his first contest as a Steeler head coach, over the Detroit Lions. The next year, the team and Noll moved on to greater things at Three Rivers Stadium. The selection here was fairly easy. Dr. Sutherland (yes, he was a doctor who graduated from the university's school of dentistry) is the clear victor. He began his career as head coach in 1924, the year before Pitt Stadium opened, and over fifteen seasons was 111-20-12 with five national championships. It was a tough selection between Jackie Sherrill and Johnny Majors, but despite the fact that Majors won a national title, Sherrill was 50-9-1 with three consecutive 11-win seasons and the 1980 *New York Times* Computer National Championship. Majors did have to deal with his second tenure at Pitt, when he was 12-32. A disciple of Sutherland, Michelosen led Pitt to two bowl games and a no. 3 ranking in 1963. Buddy Parker was the Steelers' head coach when they moved into Pitt Stadium. He led them to the second-best era of Steeler football to that point. Sutherland had led them to their best in 1946 and 1947.

GREATEST FOOTBALL COACHES IN WESTERN PENNSYLVANIA

1. Jock Sutherland
2. Chuck Noll
3. Bill Cowher
4. Mike Tomlin
5. Chuck Klausing

It was a close one here, but Sutherland's worst year at Pitt was his first (5-3-1), and his cumulative record at Pitt of losing just 20 games in 15 seasons, coupled with the fact that he won five national titles and led the Steelers to their lone postseason spot in their first forty seasons, puts him over the edge. Noll won four Super Bowls but also had some difficult seasons. Cowher and Tomlin really could be 3A and 3B, but while Tomlin has never had a losing season to this point in his career and has a better regular-season winning percentage, Cowher has been better in the playoffs, and his Hall-of-Fame selection puts him over the top. There were many candidates for the fifth spot, including Pop Warner, Jackie Sherrill and Johnny Majors, but Klausing was incredible wherever he went. He had a 124-25-2 mark at the Indiana University of Pennsylvania (IUP) and Carnegie Mellon, with eight conference titles at IUP and four playoff spots at CMU, with two Final Four appearances. He had a record of 54-0-1 at Braddock High School and six consecutive Western Pennsylvania Interscholastic Athletic League championships. All of this and his selection to the College Football Hall of Fame justify his fifth-place position.

GREATEST COACHES/MANAGERS IN WESTERN PENNSYLVANIA HISTORY

1. Jock Sutherland
2. Chuck Noll
3. Fred Clarke
4. Danny Murtaugh
5. Scotty Bowman

The reasons for choosing Jock Sutherland over Chuck Noll were given in the preceding section and remain consistent here. Fred Clarke was the

Arguably the greatest manager in Pittsburgh Pirate history, Fred Clarke (*pictured*) helped christen Forbes Field in 1909 by leading his team to its first World Series title. Overall, he was 1,422-969 in sixteen seasons as a Pirate manager, with four NL pennants and a World Series title. *Courtesy of the Pittsburgh Pirates.*

greatest manager in Pittsburgh Pirate history, winning four National League pennants in nine seasons and the franchise's first World Series title, in 1909. Danny Murtaugh was a close second, capturing four Eastern Division championships and two World Series titles, in 1960 and 1971. The fifth spot was a close decision, between two Penguin coaches. Mike Sullivan is the only coach in franchise history to lead the team to two Stanley Cup titles, but their problems winning a playoff series the past couple of years, coupled with the fact that Bowman won a Stanley Cup and drove the Pens to their greatest regular season ever in his two seasons gives him the nod here.

So there you have it. Jock Sutherland was not only the greatest coach in Pitt Stadium history but also the best the city has ever seen.

26

ON THE HEELS OF A NATIONAL TRAGEDY

The 1963 Pitt–Penn State Matchup

By David Finoli

In 1962, the University of Pittsburgh Panthers football team was an unremarkable 5-5, and there was little thought that they'd improve much on that mark a year later. But they were able to do that and then some in what was arguably the most shocking season in the program's history.

Pitt began the year with a sweep of Pac 8 opponents, defeating UCLA, Washington and Cal. After defeating WVU in the "Backyard Brawl," the Panthers stood at 4-0 as they traveled to Navy to face the tenth-ranked Midshipmen and their star quarterback, Roger Staubach. They were defeated by Navy, 24–12, in what turned out to be their only loss of the season. A great core group led by quarterback Fred Mazurek, running back Rick Leeson, Marty Schottenheimer and All-Americans Paul Martha and Ernie Borghetti pushed Pitt to victories over Syracuse, Notre Dame and Army. They found themselves at 7-1 with only Miami (Florida) and Penn State left to play. A bid to a major bowl seemed likely, with still a slim chance at a national championship. Then it happened: the day those who were around then would never forget. It was November 22, 1963. President Kennedy was shot and killed as his motorcade traveled through Dallas.

The nation was in shock, and various sports were struggling with the question of whether or not to play on the upcoming weekend. The NFL decided to play, a decision that the league's commissioner, Pete Rozelle, would later regret. But the colleges decided to hold off out of respect. It was a decision that would end up hurting the Panthers. They defeated the Hurricanes, 31–20, the next week, but the game they were originally scheduled to play that weekend was pushed back two weeks. Not wanting to gamble that Pitt would lose that contest, the bowl committees instead issued bids to other schools, costing the Panthers a shot at a title and a historic tenth victory. It was a tough circumstance, but Pitt would get past it. Instead, they faced off in what was arguably the greatest game in the long rivalry between Pitt and Penn State. It turned out to be a wonderful yet tragic victory for Pitt.

Statistically, the third-ranked Panthers thoroughly dominated play, outgaining the underdog Nittany Lions 421–279 in total yards and 310–128 on the ground. But Penn State found a way to keep the game close. Schottenheimer had a tough beginning of the game, as the Lions caught him out of position twice, one leading to a 68-yard screen pass and a second putting the visitors on top, 7–0, on a Penn State touchdown, silencing the Pitt Stadium crowd of 52,349.

After Pitt took advantage of a poor Penn State punt to come within one point at 7–6, a Mazurek fumble set up a 9-yard touchdown pass to Gerry Sandusky and a surprising 14–6 Penn State lead. Before the half, the Pitt quarterback led the Panthers on an 80-yard drive, highlighted by a 34-yard pass to Leeson and a 16-yard completion to Martha. Leeson went in from the 1 for the score, but a second failed two-point conversion left the Panthers down, 14–12, at the half.

Leeson gave the home team its first lead of the day with a 35-yard field goal, but by the time the third quarter ended, the Nittany Lions had scored again to put them up, 21–15. With the clock winding down and Pitt's incredible season in peril, the Panthers once again drove down the field and were at the Penn State 17 when Mazurek dropped back to pass. He couldn't find anyone, so he took off running. By the time he was done, he had crossed the end zone to tie the contest at 21 before Leeson's extra point gave Pitt a 1-point lead.

The underdogs would not give up and drove to the Pitt 20 before the Panther defense finally stopped them. Penn State kicker Ron Coates lined up for the go-ahead field goal with 1:29 left in the contest. Luckily for the home team, the kick sailed wide. Pitt hung on for the exciting 22–21 victory.

After the game, the Panthers were offered a conciliatory bowl bid and were asked to play in the Sun Bowl. They wanted to play Navy in a major bowl. Since this wasn't what they wanted, the school declined the bid and finished the season 9-1, ranked third in the country after this exciting game that no one really wanted to play.

III

THE FITZGERALD FIELD HOUSE
(1951–PRESENT)

REPLACING THE ICE BOX

The History of the Fitzgerald Field House

By David Finoli

When the Pitt Pavilion opened on New Year's Eve in 1925, it was hailed as one of the great basketball facilities in the country. By the time it was ready to close twenty-six years later, in 1951, it was apparent that there hadn't been too many good basketball facilities in 1925. As it turned out, the arena located below the ramps at Pitt Stadium was anything but great. It was so cold that players kept their warmup uniforms on as long as they could, and fans rarely if ever removed their coats. The visitors' locker room was outside the facility. Visiting players had to run from the cold into the stadium. The Pavilion was dirty and uncomfortable. By 1951, it was time for a new home.

The book *Pitt: 100 Years of Pitt Basketball,* written by esteemed Pitt historian Sam Sciullo Jr., includes a quote from famed *Pittsburgh Press* writer Chet Smith that held nothing back in Smith's disdain for the Pavilion. "There were no tears last night when they locked the doors on the Pitt Stadium Basketball Pavilion and threw away the keys. The Panthers Black Hole of Calcutta, home of Dr. Red [another of Carlson's nicknames] Carlson's teams since the early 1920's, can now go back to what it was originally intended to be—a cellar under the stadium. The Doctor and his boys will move into a sumptuous new field house next year."

Iconic writer Roy McHugh pointed out in a *Pittsburgh Press* column on December 14, 1951, that while the team "had moved from the slums to Park Avenue" in going from the Pitt Pavilion to the new facility, there was an intimacy to the Pavilion that most likely could not be replicated in the new facility. He told of several stories involving fans and the game, including one in which a women actually helped Pitt win a game against Notre Dame. She pulled the timer's gun from his hand so he couldn't shoot it as Pitt's Tim Lowrey put up what would be the game-winning bucket in a 1-point victory. (Yes, a gun was used at the end of each quarter and half and at the end of games.)

The Pavilion was intimate, but it was also cold—damned cold. The nickname "Ice Box" was perfect. In the same McHugh column, Panther Hall of Fame coach Doc Carlson is quoted: "The spectators functioned as their own thermometers. They could tell how cold it was by how much their anatomies turned blue."

It was more than time for a new facility. It was originally planned to be called the Memorial Field House before later being named after Pitt chancellor Rufus Fitzgerald, the man in charge of the university when the arena was built. Ground was broken on a cold day the year before with the vision of an incredible multipurpose venue. Hall-of-Fame athletic director Tom Hamilton wanted to build a place where he could house not only his basketball program but other sports as well, including wrestling and indoor track.

McHugh said that the Field House was "resplendent and modern, is quite the last word in luxurious surroundings." The hope for Fitzgerald, who understood the importance of sports and had reinstituted athletic scholarships at Pitt, was that they could improve all their programs with the Field House. But McHugh pointed out something that was more important with a state-of-the-art facility. "One change leads to another and I have the feeling that bigger and better basketball players will presently start enrolling at Pitt."

When the doors opened on December 15, 1951, it wasn't to play a soft opponent in order to get a dominant victory. It was against the powerful Columbia Lions, the defending champions of the East in college basketball. The team was in the midst of a thirty-two-game regular-season winning streak. On a frigid winter evening, 3,378 fans showed up to open the $1.3 million arena.

In the pregame ceremony, Fitzgerald, Hamilton, Field House architect William Trimble, Columbia athletic director Ralph Furey and several other dignitaries, including former Pitt football greats Dr. J Huber Wagner, Clair Cribbs and Don Smith, gave speeches. Hamilton presented the team's legendary coach, Doc Carlson, with a dedication basketball. While the favorites dominated early, going into the half with a 38–31 lead, Pitt fought back in the second half but fell behind by 7 once again, 62–55, late in the contest. The Panthers refused to give up, and Bernie Artman drove in for the winning basket late in a shocking 65–64 upset.

While Pitt didn't immediately build the winning programs that Hamilton had envisioned, the Panther basketball team went on to enjoy an elite eight seasons beginning in 1973–74 before becoming a force in the Eastern Eight, winning back-to-back tournament crowns in 1981 and 1982. They then won in the powerful Big East with regular-season titles in 1987 and 1988. In total, playing in the Fitzgerald Field House, the Panther men's basketball program secured twelve bids to the NCAA tournament, and the women captured the 1984 Big East regular-season crown. Alongside Pitt basketball, the arena was also home to the Duquesne Dukes men's basketball team between 1956 and 1964, giving it a home after the Duquesne Gardens was razed. The Panthers stayed there until 2002, when the Petersen Events Center was completed.

As the university enters the third decade of the twenty-first century, current Pitt athletic director Heather Lyke has helped guide the school to the vision Hamilton had seventy years earlier. The Fitzgerald Field House is the only one of the four Oakland historic facilities celebrated in this book that is still active. It now houses the gymnastics team as well as women's volleyball and men's wrestling.

Wrestling has been arguably the most successful program at the Field House over the years, with sixteen individual national champions, eleven conference championships, eighty All-Americans and three wrestling Hall of Famers. The program finished ranked eleventh in the country following the 2020–21 campaign. The gymnastics team captured the 2016 East Atlantic Gymnastic League championship, and women's volleyball battles with men's soccer as the most successful program on campus.

Achieving the volleyball program's highest national ranking in 2019, when they found themselves second in the nation in the coaches' poll, they have also captured nine regular-season championships while being invited to the national championship tournament on nineteen occasions. Their best finish was an Final Four appearance in the 2022 tournament.

In January 2020, Lyke announced her Victory Height's athletic plan, which included a new 3,500-seat arena for gymnastics, volleyball and wrestling. The days of the Field House are numbered. A *Pittsburgh Sports Now* article by Alan Saunders on January 14, 2020, quoted Lyke as saying: "For far too long, a significant percentage of our student-athletes have been forced to compete in facilities that do not reflect the lofty standards and aspirations of the University of Pittsburgh." In essence, the Field House is old and needs to be replaced. It's the same thought Hamilton had about the Pitt Pavilion sixty-nine years earlier.

When the time comes for the Fitzgerald Field House to be eliminated, the university can be proud of the fact that it made Tom Hamilton's vision come true. It was a place where the school housed winning programs.

BUILDING A CHAMPIONSHIP PROGRAM AT THE FITZGERALD FIELD HOUSE

Pitt Volleyball

By David Finoli

When one thinks of national championship–caliber programs at the University of Pittsburgh, they think of the football program at Pitt Stadium led by Pop Warner, Jock Sutherland, Johnny Majors and Jackie Sherrill. As the 2010s were coming to an end and the 2020s were emerging, two more programs were beginning to bloom. One was men's soccer. It became the first Pitt athletic program to go to an NCAA tournament Final Four since men's basketball achieved the feat in 1941. The other plays under the Fitzgerald Field House roof and has been the most consistent winning team between 2016 and 2022: Pitt women's volleyball.

Creating a championship culture is difficult. It's why so many coaches get fired on an annual basis. The school found its man to create such a culture when it hired Dan Fisher following the 2012 campaign. After leading Concordia College to the NAIA national championship in 2012, he was hired to lead the Panthers into a new era as they joined the Atlantic Coast Conference (ACC). The team was selected to finish thirteenth in the ACC preseason poll and ended up with a winning record in the conference at 11-9, fifth place. Championship cultures need a building block, and this was the one for Pitt volleyball.

The team improved to 25-6 in 2014 and 23-9 a year later, both seasons with matching 13-7 ACC marks. In 2016, they went 15-5 in the conference

Pictured is the volleyball court at the Fitzgerald Field House. The court is now home to the consistently most successful athletic program on a campus. The volleyball squad has become a perennial top-twenty team and, in 2022, made it to the Final Four of the NCAA tournament. *Courtesy of the University of Pittsburgh Athletics.*

while garnering their first NCAA tournament appearance in twelve years, advancing to the second round. Pitt captured 26 wins in 2017 with a co-ACC championship and a second consecutive NCAA appearance. As good as it had been, the program still hadn't taken the step to national-championship contender. Fisher was about to lead the program to a level it had never seen.

In 2018, the pieces of a championship culture were falling into place. The squad won all but one conference game and their first outright ACC title and a 17-1 conference mark. Fisher, who won his 200th contest at Pitt in September 2021, led his team to a remarkable 30-2 mark with a school record .938 winning percentage. They were ranked seventh in the final RPI poll and received a twelfth seed for their third consecutive NCAA appearance. With the seed came home matches in the first and second round of the tournament. These games were moved from their home court at the Field House to the larger Petersen Event Center. They easily defeated Iona, 3–0, in the first round but unfortunately had their season cut short with a 3–2 loss to Michigan in round two.

The next season, the team had cruised to a 21-1 mark when the program hit a height it had never seen. In late October, after top-ranked Baylor was defeated by Texas, Pitt shot up to no. 2 in the country on the AVCA coaches' poll. They ended up undefeated in ACC play for their third consecutive conference title, staying second in the poll for six consecutive weeks. Once again, the team was given home-court advantage in the NCAA tournament. And, as in 2018, the games were moved to the Petersen Events Center.

In the first round, they were dominant against Howard, earning a 3–0 victory. They then faced a team they had beaten in the regular season, the Cincinnati Bearcats. To this point in the program's history, the Panthers had made the second round seven times but unfortunately lost every time. This was their chance to finally take the next step. With a nineteen-match winning streak intact and an anticipated matchup in the Sweet Sixteen against their bitter rivals from Penn State on the line, that mark unfortunately turned to 0-8 with a stunning 3–2 loss against the Bearcats.

It got worse, as the fall portion of the Panthers' 2020–21 campaign ended with a mediocre 4-4 mark. When the program began the 2021 portion of its schedule after an almost four-month layoff due to COVID, it won 12 consecutive victories and landed a fifth consecutive NCAA bid. Because of COVID, the entire tournament was played in Omaha. Perhaps playing off campus was what the team needed. After an opening-round sweep of Long Island University, they swept no. 14 Utah to finally get beyond the second round. The Panthers then faced third-ranked Minnesota in the

Sweet Sixteen. They upset the Gophers in five grueling sets, 3–2, to take on the University of Washington in the Elite Eight. After winning the first two sets, they unfortunately dropped the final three. But they had finally taken the program to a place where they could now envision a national championship.

In 2021, the Panthers got off to a top-five start, eventually rising to second by midseason. They eventually reached the Final Four before a disappointing loss against number 10 Nebraska. They are playing to packed crowds in the Field House. They have become perennial national-championship contenders, something no other team that ever played in the Fitzgerald Field House could claim.

29

THE PEERY DYNASTY AND THE 1957 NCAA WRESTLING CHAMPIONSHIPS

By David Finoli

While many coaches and wrestlers have made the University of Pittsburgh's program one of the most consistently successful at the university, one family in particular made the program special, beginning in 1949, when Rex Peery took over coaching. Peery had been an excellent wrestler in college, capturing three NCAA titles while at Oklahoma A&M (now Oklahoma State). His two sons, Ed and Hugh Peery, joined him at the school. Hugh captured three titles between 1952 and 1954. The younger brother, Ed, won NCAA championships his sophomore and junior seasons (1955 and 1956). In 1957, Ed was a senior at the school and was looking to match his father and brother. The NCAA brought its wrestling championship to the Fitzgerald Field House that year to see if the youngest Peery could complete the family's remarkable achievement.

Pitt had twice tried wrestling in the past and twice had failed before Athletic Director Tom Hamilton looked to the most successful program in the country and brought the elder Peery to lead the Panther program. Led by Rex's sons, Pitt had immediate success. They won four consecutive Eastern crowns before finishing second to Penn State in the Eastern tournament shortly before the NCAAs began. They had finished ninth, sixth, second, third and third in the previous five national tournaments.

Hamilton was the person responsible for convincing the NCAA to bring its tournament to the Field House in 1957. While fans in the city have seen several NCAA championships in various sports since the late 1990s, this one was the first to be awarded to Pittsburgh. It was the biggest event at the time, with a record sixty-one teams coming to town.

As excitement for the upcoming tournament grew, the focus of most wrestling fans was on the youngest Peery. Could he match his father and brother with a third championship at 123 pounds? It wouldn't be easy. There were many good wrestlers at that weight class, including Dick Mueller of Minnesota, who had captured the class in the 1953 tournament before being drafted into the Korean conflict.

Oklahoma was the heavy favorite to win the national championship, but there was enough talent at Pitt that they hoped to finish right behind the Sooners. The Panthers were deep, with Ed Peery, Dave Johnson, Ron Schirf (Johnson and Schirf winning Eastern championships) and Tom Alberts, who wrestled at 167 pounds and had been declared academically ineligible for the Eastern championships. But he corrected whatever grade deficiency he had and was able to wrestle in the nationals.

As the tourney went on, Pitt was hanging with Oklahoma and had five wrestlers in the semifinals. The four men already mentioned qualified, as did Bill Hullings at 115. As it turned out, Alberts and Schirf won national championships. Johnson lost in the semifinals, and Hullings dropped a decision to the Sooners' Dick Delgado in the finals. That left Peery, who was trying to make history against Harmon Leslie of Oklahoma A&M.

An enthusiastic crowd of 4,554 filled the Field House in what turned out to be one of the most difficult matches in Ed Peery's career. He was down, 7–6, late in the match when he was given a point for what is referred to as riding time, given to the wrestler who the referee feels dominated the match. Tied, 7–7, the two men went into overtime, where Ed once again received a point for riding time. The match was now tied, 2–2, in overtime.

The rule at the time was to have three officials vote to award the match to one of the wrestlers instead of having another overtime. They felt that Peery was the dominant wrestler and awarded him his historic third title.

Pitt was phenomenal, finishing with 66 points, second behind the Sooners' 73 and far ahead of their rivals, the Nittany Lions, who were third with 38 points. The other memorable moment of the tournament came when Iowa's Simon Roberts became the first African American to capture a national title. Among all of the notable achievements, for Pitt fans, Ed Peery matching his dad's and brother's feat with a third national championship was something to cherish.

30

"SEND IT IN JEROME"

Jerome Lane's Famous Backboard-Breaking Moment

By David Finoli

There was a lot going on for the Pitt basketball program when the team met the Providence Friars on January 25, 1988. They had started the season with a nine-game winning streak before frustrating losses to Georgetown and Oklahoma, who defeated the Panthers, 86–83, the game before this one, and Pitt stood at 13-2 coming into this contest. Despite the two losses, the Panthers were one of the best teams in the country, remaining in the top twenty-five all season and capturing a no. 2 seed in the NCAA tournament. The Friars were no match for the Panthers, as the 34-point differential in the 90–56 final score indicates. So why is the game remembered as arguably the most memorable moment in the long history of the Fitzgerald Field House? It was because of a six-foot, one-inch power forward by the name of Jerome Lane, whose monstrous backboard-breaking dunk is still talked about with reverence four decades later.

Lane was a unique player. Not one of the biggest forwards on the floor, he made himself one of the best rebounders in the country, outperforming players much bigger than himself and becoming the shortest player to lead the nation in that stat in almost thirty years. He was the epitome of a power forward and, on this evening, would show the basketball world just how powerful he was.

Here's how the play set up. Future Xavier coach Sean Miller was a freshman point guard for the Panthers on this evening. With his team only up by 1 point early in the game, he picked off an errant Providence inbound pass. He saw he had a three-on-one break going toward the Pitt basket and chose Lane to pass to, knowing he'd finish the play. What Miller didn't know was exactly how hard Lane was going to finish the play. Lane threw down a savage dunk that shattered the backboard. Teammate Jason Matthews said the booming sound the play made was like a brick being tossed through a big window.

While the dunk was incredible, the fact that the game was televised nationally on ESPN made it legendary. Glass rained onto the floor, and a stunned Bill Rafferty started screaming, "Ohh!" Surprised at what he saw, he then muttered the words that always accompany the play when it is shown: "Send it in Jerome."

The fans in the sellout crowd were on their feet, screaming as loud as they could. The Panther mascot took the fallen hoop and paraded it around the Fitzgerald Field House. The game had to be delayed twenty-nine minutes, and this took the moment into the stratosphere. The broadcast was sent to ESPN legend Bob Ley in the studio, and the network played the moment again and again, to the point that just about every basketball fan in the nation became aware of the amazing moment that had just taken place in the Field House.

When play resumed, the Panthers went on to a one-sided victory over Providence. Lane and Charles Smith led Pitt with 17 points each. But those 2 points early on are what the Akron, Ohio native will always be known for. It has gotten to the point that, at every milestone anniversary of the play, it becomes a national event. ESPN named it one of its one hundred greatest sports highlights.

In the history of basketball, many backboards have been broken due to thunderous dunks. But this combination of a national TV audience, a twenty-nine-minute delay that turned into a highlight celebration and a Hall-of-Fame announcer making a memorable call made this the greatest backboard-breaking dunk of all.

31

THE FORGING OF A PRESIDENT

Two Key Campaign Stops in Oakland Fuel the Legend of JFK

By Chris Fletcher

John Fitzgerald Kennedy was a generational politician. His status as the youngest man elected to the presidency, his lofty ideals and promise for a better future and his tragic assassination serving as a flashpoint for an era all combined to create a fabled time—one often more romantic than realistic.

But there would be no Camelot without Pittsburgh, specifically Oakland, where two speeches helped propel the Kennedy legend.

For JFK, Pittsburgh offered an alluring trifecta: urban minorities, ethnic voting blocs and organized labor. He was following the road map charted by Franklin Delano Roosevelt two decades before. Kennedy knew he would need these three groups in the 1960 presidential election and beyond to achieve his agenda.

The city also allowed him to tout a platform geared toward urbanism. Pittsburgh was in the midst of Renaissance I, which began shortly after World War II. Most of that progress was happening across town at the Point, where the Allegheny and Monongahela Rivers met to form the Ohio. The area had been known for run-down buildings, railroad tracks, an automobile tow pound, vacant lots and crumbling buildings. All of that was cleared to make Point State Park, which became a central gathering space for Pittsburgh.

Kennedy seized on that theme as he took the stage during a campaign stop.

Appearance One: Syria Mosque, October 10, 1960

The Kennedy Conference on Urban Affairs had just finished its Pittsburgh meeting. The report from the conference offered a damning state of the American city—forty million Americans living in substandard housing and critical shortages of affordable housing. Kennedy supported a monumental government effort to raise the standard of the nation's urban core, the type of push that had formed the backbone of the New Deal.

In a heavily Democratic stronghold, JFK was not shy about summoning the FDR mystique. "I come from Warm Springs, Georgia, this morning, the house where Franklin Roosevelt died, and I come to Pittsburgh, Pennsylvania, and invoke his spirit."

Pittsburgh provided a good backdrop to talk about plans for cleaning the environment. "America has not yet begun to combat air and water pollution in earnest," the Kennedy Conference reported. But if Pittsburgh could tackle its industrial smoke and polluted waters, so could the rest of the country. Kennedy favored a funding mechanism in which every dollar invested locally would be matched with two dollars on the federal level.

And at the Syria Mosque, he also issued a challenge to the crowd. "We could not conserve and look backward if we tried," he said. "We must look forward…and I come here to Pittsburgh and ask your help in this campaign."

His campaign swing through the region may have been the difference in an election that looked eerily like 2020. Sixty years ago, in a tight contest, Kennedy (much like Joe Biden) won Pennsylvania by carrying the urban areas of Pittsburgh and Philadelphia.

Appearance Two: Fitzgerald Field House, October 12, 1962

At what should have been the midway point of Kennedy's presidency, there was turbulence. Two weeks before his arrival in Oakland to drum up support for the Democratic ticket in the upcoming election, Kennedy had to confront a major event in the civil rights movement.

An African American college student, James Meredith, arrived at the University of Mississippi to attend class, escorted by federal marshals. A deadly riot broke out, led by an angry crowd of students and other local whites who opposed Meredith's effort to integrate "Old Miss."

Kennedy called in the military to restore order, but the event caused the president to question his administration's approach to civil rights. It would shape his Pittsburgh appearance, as he talked about what it meant to have access to higher education.

"We're meeting tonight in this distinguished university, all of us," Kennedy said. "I saw more children today, driving into this city—all of these children and all of those mothers and fathers will want those children to have an opportunity to attend this school or others like it. By 1970, we're going to have twice as many boys and girls trying to get into our colleges as were in 1960. That means that we have to build in the next 10 years as many college dormitories and buildings as we built in the whole 150-year history of our country."

Those words would be prophetic for the Oakland corridor, as Pitt and Carnegie Mellon University would flex their academic muscles over the coming decades, adding prestigious and innovative programs as well as facilities that are among the best in the collegiate ranks.

Unfortunately, JFK would never live to see those days. Two appearances in Oakland helped forge a legend and served as a what-might-have-been.

32

WHEN THE CITY GAME WAS GREAT

Pitt-Duquesne Basketball at the Field House

By Robert Healy III

Many of us are guilty of remembering the past as better than it really was. But technology and enlightenment make almost every era better for human beings than the previous one was.

There are exceptions to that, however.

If you're a fan of college basketball in Western Pennsylvania, for example, it's hard to top what the region's eminent hoops rivalry was like in the middle of the previous century, especially since the rivals no longer play each other on an annual basis and one or both teams aren't usually national powerhouses.

The City Game rivalry between Duquesne University's and the University of Pittsburgh's men's basketball teams is on hiatus, but even when it was a regular event in the twenty-first century, the matchup was not usually competitive (or entertaining), with Pitt winning—often comfortably— seventeen of the nineteen meetings since the 2000–01 season.

Pitt's and Duquesne's teams went on opposite trajectories in the early 1980s, with Pitt eventually becoming the top dog in town. The Panthers even attained a no. 1 national ranking during the 2008–09 season, the same year they trounced the Dukes in routine fashion, 78–51 at the sparkling Petersen Events Center, Pitt's relatively new facility built to house a national title contender. But in those halcyon days of yore, the City Game was much more spirited— and compelling. Pittsburgh sports fans, not as connected to the rest of the world as they are today, cared greatly about local bragging rights.

Willie Somerset (*to the left*) dribbles around a Pitt player during the City Game. Somerset was a first-team All-American and still holds the school record for points per game in a career with 22.7. *Courtesy of Duquesne University Athletics.*

To boot, while the major league Pittsburgh Civic and PPG Paints arenas have served as City Game locations, the game was once played exclusively on campus sites, which seemingly always adds to the pageantry of college sports.

Perhaps the most memorable of those campus matchups were at the Memorial (later Fitzgerald) Field House, a University of Pittsburgh building that served as the home venue for Pitt basketball from its opening in 1951 through the 2001–02 season and Duquesne basketball from the 1956–57 through 1963–64 seasons.

"When Fitzgerald is rocking…there's no better sport venue in town," the *Pittsburgh Post-Gazette*'s Bob Smizik wrote when recalling Field House memories in 2002. "No other venue puts the fans as close to the action, no other venue so intimidates the opposition."

For the 1953 through 1963 City Games, though, it was hard to determine who "the opposition" was. While the games were on Pitt's campus, the Dukes had plenty of fans willing to make the three-mile trip east from their university to root against the Panthers and for a celebrated Dukes program that, in the 1950s alone, achieved a no. 1 national ranking, won a national title and had two no. 1 picks (back to back) in the NBA Draft.

The Panthers weren't national contenders at the first two City Games at the Field House, Decembers 1953 and 1955. But in the early and mid-1950s, the Dukes definitely were, and they blew out Pitt, 79–43 and 71–49, respectively.

Those two games were part of Pitt's December Steel Bowl tournament at the Field House, as was each subsequent City Game through 1963. In 1964, the Dukes left the Field House to make the Civic Arena their full-time home, and the City Game was played as a Steel Bowl game there for a time, too. The rivals didn't wage a Field House contest again until February 1977, a 66–63 Duquesne overtime win that came as part of the school's schedule in the Eastern Collegiate Basketball League, the forerunner to the Atlantic 10 Conference that still counts the Dukes as members.

The City Game saw six other "Eastern 8" regular-season or postseason contests at the Field House, plus four nonconference tilts there after Pitt joined the Big East. But nothing seemed to match the magic of the Steel Bowl at Pitt, which also welcomed Westminster, Carnegie Tech, Geneva, Fordham, Duke and others.

Pitt got its first Steel Bowl win over Duquesne in 1956, 59–50. The Dukes won the next December, but the Pitt program began gaining on Duquesne's and won four of the final six Steel Bowl versions of the City Game at the Field House, including the last one, 69–67, in overtime for the tournament championship. Regulation ended when Pitt official timer (and maintenance worker) Leo "Horse" Czarnecki ruled that an apparent last-second field goal by Duquesne's John Cegalis did not beat the buzzer.

The all-time series for Steel Bowl City Games at the Field House stands at Duquesne five, Pitt five.

As the saying goes, some things just aren't what they used to be.

33

PLAYING LIKE NATIONAL CHAMPIONS

Pitt Cruises Past the Soon-to-Be National Champion Villanova Wildcats

By David Finoli

As the Villanova Wildcats came into the Fitzgerald Field House on March 2, 1985, they had the look of a team whose best hope for the season was an NCAA tournament bid and perhaps an unexpected run for a spot in the Sweet Sixteen. No one could have envisioned that a few weeks later they would make a miraculous run through the field of sixty-four as an eighth seed, culminating with a memorable upset win over Georgetown to capture their first NCAA national championship. They were coming into this final contest of the regular season with an 18-8 mark, 9-6 in the Big East Conference, looking to shore up a third seed in the conference tournament. A national championship was something seemingly not in the cards for Rollie Massimino and his squad of Wildcats.

The home team had a couple things to play for. They had a shot to finish with a .500 record in conference play for the first time since they joined the Big East and a chance to improve their résumé in hopes of an at-large bid to March Madness. No one expected what happened next. The big, bad Wildcats threw up the white flag, giving up early in the second half, while the Panthers looked like a team on the verge of big things. On this day, Pitt was playing like national champions.

Massimino had ridden his big three players hard during the regular season. Ed Pinckney, Dwayne McClain and Harold Pressley had all logged over thirty-three minutes per game during the regular season. Playing so much over a long period of time had to be draining to the three players. On this afternoon, in front of a sold-out Fitzgerald Field House, that's exactly what appeared to be happening.

Pinckney was struggling the most, going scoreless until hitting two free throws with under three minutes left in the first half as the Panthers went into the locker room with a stunning 40–23 lead. An article by Steve Halvonik of the *Pittsburgh Press* quoted the Wildcat coach: "I thought Pitt played outstanding. They shot well and were aggressive. They really went after it. We were a little lethargic. That's why the score was the way it was." Probably the biggest understatement in his quote was claiming they were a "little" lethargic. He should have said "extremely," and Rollie knew it. That's why he threatened to pull his starting squad after three minutes in the second half if they did not improve. They did not.

Pitt came out of the locker room with an even greater intensity. They ripped Villanova with an 18-6 advantage to start the second half, making the score 58–29. At that point, Massimino did exactly what he threatened to do: pull his starters and leave the game to his bench. The humiliating contest was on national TV, as CBS was broadcasting the Saturday afternoon affair. Rollie seemingly gave up, and that was not exactly taken well. In a column by Gene Collier in the *Press* that day, he quoted Panther associate athletic director Dean Billick: "I would hesitate to tell Rollie how to coach his basketball team, but from a league point of view, it might not have been in the best interests of the league, especially on national television. He did everything but throw up the white flag."

Pitt went on to finish the destruction with an 85–62 victory and looked like a team on the rise. Many wondered if Villanova's season would end with early losses in both the Big East and NCAA tourneys. That's when things turned around dramatically for Massimino. He beat Pitt in the Big East quarterfinals, 69–61, and went on an unprecedented run through the NCAA tournament, defeating second-ranked Michigan, seventh-ranked North Carolina and fifth-ranked Memphis State and shocking the no. 1 team in the nation, Georgetown, 66–64, in arguably the greatest upset in an NCAA finals matchup.

The Panthers did end up getting their first NCAA bid as a member of the Big East, but unlike Villanova, their national championship hopes ended in the first round with a 78–54 loss to Louisiana Tech. Regardless of how the two seasons ended, on this afternoon, Pitt had the looks of a national champion with one of the most impressive wins they ever had at the Field House.

34

A BIG EAST BAPTISM

Pitt Upsets St. Johns

By David Finoli

As the 1980s began, the University of Pittsburgh basketball program had finally taken itself up the Eastern Eight ladder (the former name of the Atlantic 10 Conference). They had gone from a struggling member in the league's infancy to one of the premier programs, winning the conference tournament in 1981 and 1982 and with it an automatic bid to the NCAA tournament. The program was looking for bigger and better things when it moved to one of the elite conferences in college basketball, the Big East, to begin the 1982–83 campaign. There would be growing pains for sure, and not much was expected of Dr. Roy Chipman's team that first season. They had done OK up to this point, with a 2-5 conference mark. But following an exciting double-overtime win against Providence at the Fitzgerald Field House, they took on one of the most powerful teams in the country, the St. John's Redmen. They had played three ranked Big East teams to this point and had been soundly beaten by all of them. St. John's was the best of the group, so most were expecting a relatively easy affair. The Redmen got more than they bargained for in the end, as Pitt secured its first headline victory in the conference.

Coming into the game, St. John's had won eighteen of nineteen games, losing only to Boston College, and while he never admitted it out loud, Hall of Famer Lou Carnesecca thought he'd easily make it 19-1. They were ranked fourth in the country in the United Press International poll and fifth by the Associated Press. Led by the great Chris Mullin, Billy

Goodwin and center Bill Wennington, St. John's had a suffocating man-to-man defense that caused huge issues offensively for teams superior to the talent Pitt had. As the game began, it looked exactly like the rout everyone predicted, with the Redmen leading, 15–7. At that point, a frustrated Chipman called a timeout.

Pitt had lost some close conference games at this point and wanted nothing more than to prove they could play tough against the best the Big East had to offer. Coming out of break, the Panthers did just that. They were able to get past the seven-foot Wennington and six-foot, ten-inch center Jeff Allen with relative ease all of a sudden and outscored the Redmen, 25–16, after the timeout to go into the locker room with a stunning 32–31 lead. There was still twenty minutes left in the game, and a Pitt victory was still a long shot. Could they continue the intensity the rest of the way?

The Fitzgerald Field House was sold out, with 6,180 on hand. The crowd was loud as they saw the underdog home team continuing to play well against the fourth-ranked Redmen. As regulation was coming to an end and St. John's had a 1-point lead, Billy Culbertson stole the ball from Mullin and drove in with a layup to put the Panthers back ahead, 56–55.

With time running out, Pitt continued to be aggressive and draw fouls. They ended the game by going 28 for 35 from the line, compared to St. John's 11 of 15. Andre Williams and Clyde Vaughan led the way and were almost perfect in free throws with a combined 20 for 21, each scoring a team-high 24 points. With under a minute left, the Panthers held a 71–69 advantage as the Redmen possessed the ball with one last chance to win. Goodwin dribbled down with fifteen seconds left and, instead of working the ball inside, where the visitors had a size advantage, he put up a shot that Culbertson rebounded and ended up hitting the front end of a one-on-one, putting the Panthers in front by 3. Goodwin scored on a layup with time running out, but it was too little, too late. The Panthers had their upset.

Carnesecca didn't want to make any excuses for the loss. In an article for New York's *Newsday* by Paul Smith, the Hall-of-Fame coach said: "No, please, it wasn't the Field House. It was not a disaster. The world will go on—you're going to kick some away, particularly in this league." But for Pitt and its fans, it was a special win, a baptism in the Big East Conference, where the team did in fact prove that it could play with anyone.

35

WHAT A COACH SHOULD BE

Pitt Wrestling Coach Rande Stottlemyer

By David Finoli

As we grow up, we hear what some say the perfect coach should be. Disciplined, tough on players, demanding perfection. If they don't have these characteristics and win, we as fans demand that they be fired. In reality, this isn't what a good coach is, especially at the college level and below. Yes, winning is part of the equation. Winning generates revenue, and revenue is needed for sports programs to exist. But good coaching is more than that. Does the coach make the athlete better? Does he or she instill discipline that makes players not only successful on the field of play but also in the classroom and in life? Do they help make the players successful off the field? If you talk to the athletes who wrestled for Pitt wrestling coach Rande Stottlemyer, they say their coach checked all the boxes. He was what a coach is supposed to be.

Stottlemyer began his love affair with Pitt in the late 1970s as a three-time All-American for the Panthers, sporting a 68-16-2 mark with one Eastern Wrestling League (EWL) championship. He was so intense in wanting to be the best that after injuring his ankle, he ran around the track at the Field House with crutches so he could stay in shape instead of sitting and trying to recover.

A captain for each of his varsity seasons at the school, Rande graduated in 1978, taking a job as Pitt coach Dave Adams's assistant the next season. A year later, he was named the school's head coach and remained there for thirty-four years before retiring in 2013 at fifty-seven, leaving a legacy

Legendary Pitt wrestling coach Rande Stottlemyer *(far left)* stands with three of his wrestlers. With Coach Stottlemeyer, are, from left to right, Kyle Nellis, John Hnath and Gary Bolin. *Courtesy of Gary Bolin.*

that has been unrivaled by most coaches at the school. He retired with a 304-231-12 mark as head coach, having produced fifty-six EWL individual champions, thirty-three All-Americans and three national champions. In his last four campaigns, he produced three EWL regular-season team titles and three consecutive EWL team tournament championships. Pitt finished fifteenth in the nation his final two years. With his impressive résumé, he was arguably the greatest coach to grace the sidelines at the Fitzgerald Field House. But Stottlemyer was more than just a coach who knew how to win. To his wrestlers, he was much more than that.

Pat Santoro, the four-time All-American at Pitt who won national championships in 1988 and 1989 and went on to a successful coaching career at Maryland and Lehigh, said: "Rande has been one of the most influential people in my life. He took a chance on me with very few accolades and believed he could help me develop, and he was right. I am very grateful that I was able to wrestle for him, be mentored by him and later calling him my friend. Rande was a man of strong character and faith, and transformed lives long after his student athletes left Pitt. There could not have been a better person to be around at such a key time in my life. I know that I am just one of many that feel the same way."

Gary Bolin wrestled for Pitt between 1982 and 1987, winning the EWL championship at 142 pounds in 1985 and 1986 while being named captain of the team twice. While those were impressive parts of his career, what he remembers most is the effect his coach had on his time at Pitt and on his life.

"I remember when I was a senior in high school, he came to my house and he was just a very likable guy. He was so approachable and very much a family man. If I could describe him in one word it would be loyal. Loyal to his family and loyal to his wrestlers. He was humble but had a lot of charisma also. He was an easy guy to get to know. I couldn't wait to wrestle for a guy that was so down to earth. He made you feel comfortable being around him because he was so well rounded. He was focused on you as an individual and knowing what was important in life. It was those type of qualities that attracted me to Rande and the program."

Bolin was inspired by Stottlemyer's work ethic and attention to detail when it came to the wrestling mat. "He was always engaged with you in the wrestling room. He was always right in the mix of things. He was there running with you at the Field House at 6:00 a.m. or lifting with you. It made us want to make him proud in the matches."

As good as Stottlemyer was teaching them to be their best when they wrestled, Bolin recalled a saying the legendary coach told his athletes that he takes with him in his life today. "I still live by a saying that he often said. He always told us 'don't let your highs get you too high and your lows get you too low.' I learned this when I used to wrestle at Pitt but I also learned this is true through life. You're going to go through ups and downs in life, and I've lived with this throughout my life, whether it's at work or my family and back then in sports."

Unfortunately, Stottlemyer didn't retire because he felt he had achieved everything he wanted to. It was because the signs of early-onset Alzheimer's were beginning to appear. Bolin said: "He retired because of the symptoms of Alzheimer's disease. It came on really early in his life at fifty-seven, and he passed away five years later in 2018. Otherwise he'd probably still be there [coaching Pitt]."

Even though he was challenged by it, the coach who was awarded the National Wrestling Hall of Fame's Lifetime Achievement Award didn't stop being a part of the program. He continued to show up at the matches with his wife. Bolin remembered Rande's wife, Regina, saying, "This just kept him going mentally even though he knew he had to retire from coaching, and it helped him with his overall health."

Finally, on January 28, 2018, Rande passed away at the young age of sixty-two. He was so loved by his wrestlers and others he touched over the years that many came to a service to celebrate his life. Gary recalled one speaker in particular, Boyd Shrum, a dear friend of the Pitt coach, who talked about a conversation he and Stottlemyer had as they were coming back from a long trip. Even though Stottlemyer was showing signs of dementia, Rande talked to him about what was special about his wife and four children. Shrum made mental notes and talked about this at the service. It showed that no matter how sick he was, Rande's love for his family was always at the forefront of his thoughts.

Bolin confided that one of the coach's favorite sayings was, "I hate these long goodbyes," and he went on to talk about the irony of suffering from a disease that really is a long goodbye.

While the end of his life may have been cruel, the love Rande's wrestlers show for him is proof of his greatness. He was truly what a coach should be.

36

COUNTRY'S NO. 2 TEAM FALLS TO DUQUESNE AT PITT FIELD HOUSE

By Robert Healy III

T he Duquesne basketball team is gambling its whole season on the outcome of one game today," United Press International's Martin Lader wrote about the March 1, 1961 Duquesne matchup against St. Bonaventure, the Associated Press' no. 2–ranked team in the nation, "but even the Dukes must be wondering if they've inadvertently chosen the wrong team on the wrong night."

The Dukes had chosen the Bonaventure game at the University of Pittsburgh Field House, the Dukes' home court since the Duquesne Gardens had closed in 1956, as their chance to prove they belonged in the 1961 National Invitation Tournament (NIT). The players even wrote a letter about it to NIT selection chair Ken Norton. "In brief," Lader wrote, "the letter read: 'We are resting our case on the Bonnie game.…All that we ask is that you give us serious consideration after reading the papers on March 2.'"

The NIT is hardly as appealing these days as the NCAA tournament is, but in 1961, playing under the bright lights of New York City's Madison Square Garden was quite alluring. New York media told the stories of programs like Duquesne's to a nationwide audience. To boot, the NIT, especially in its initial years, was not a consolation event. And the NCAA champion wasn't always universally thought of as being the country's best team. The NIT, which is now a property of the NCAA, predates the NCAA tournament and rivaled it—at least somewhat—until 1970. That year, the AP's eighth-ranked team, Marquette, opted for the NIT instead of the NCAA tournament.

So, in 1961, for a school like Duquesne, 1955 NIT champions but having gone without an appearance in any postseason tournament since 1956, a return to the esteemed New York event would also mark a return to the program's glory days.

But the unranked Dukes were substantial underdogs, despite the Bonnies coming off of "a shocking upset," Lader wrote, at home to Niagara the game before. St. Bonaventure had also lost to top-ranked and eventual NCAA runner-up Ohio State that season, but by only 2 points.

Duquesne also lost to Niagara, 58–53, at home.

"Somewhat humiliated, St. Bonaventure is out for revenge," Lader wrote, "and Duquesne stands directly in the path."

The Dukes' only other shot at the Bonnies that season, an 89–78 road loss, came on January 7, when the AP had St. Bonaventure ranked no. 3.

The Dukes staked their reputation, though, on the outcome of their rematch at home against the Bonnies, already bound for the NCAA tournament.

The Bonnies caught wind of the letter, and so too must have Dukes fans. A standing-room audience of 5,439, according to the Duquesne record book, crowded into the Field House and was treated to a dandy.

Bob Slobodnik put the Dukes up late, 63–60, but a pair of layups by first-team AP All-American Tom Stith, who finished with 19 points, followed to put the Bonnies ahead by 1. Fred Crawford, who led his team that night with 29 points, then made a free throw to bump the lead to 2, and that set the stage for Slobodnik, who finished with 16 points, to put the game into overtime at 65–65 via a jumper with twenty seconds left. St. Bonaventure's Bob McCully almost won it, but his potential game-winning shot came just after the buzzer to end regulation, officials ruled.

Clyde Arnold, who also had 16 points, put the Dukes ahead for good when his 3 straight points made it 72–69. Duquesne's Ned Twyman, whom the AP called "a ball of fire throughout [the game]," scored 6 of his game-high 31 points in overtime, and when the final score showed 79–74, that set off a raucous celebration by Dukes fans.

"The scene on the basketball floor after last night's Duquesne win over St. Bonaventure resembled the hysterical mobs that roamed the city streets when the Pirates won the World Series last fall," the *Pittsburgh Press*' Bob Drum reported. "The students thundered out of the stands and mobbed the five men who played the whole way, including overtime, for the Dukes."

The result was so exciting for Duquesne that its president, Reverend Henry J. McAnulty, canceled the next day's classes.

Sadly for the Dukes, the NIT nevertheless passed on them in 1961, but the win over Bonaventure, the highest-ranked team Duquesne has ever beaten, started a season-ending four-game winning streak and spurred the Dukes to a 22-7 record in 1961–62, including a fourth-place finish in the NIT.

37

GOING OUT IN STYLE

Duquesne Perfect in Last Two Years at Home at Pitt Field House

By Robert Healy III

It's hard to top undefeated.

According to the Duquesne University men's basketball official record book, the only legitimate home venue in the team's history (through the 2020–21 season) without a loss is the very new UPMC Cooper Fieldhouse. The venue—if you consider it to be unique to its predecessor, the A.J. Palumbo Center, which shared most of the same real estate—opened in February 2021 during a crazy, COVID-19-affected season and has hosted just two games, a 69–64 win over the rival Dayton Flyers and an 86–75 triumph over the Rhode Island Rams.

Combine those wins with a 1-0 mark for the Duquesne women at the new facility (through 2020–21), and you can safely say "the Coop" has been friendly confines so far for the university's hoops programs.

While the Cooper Fieldhouse has made quite a first impression on Dukes fans, there is arguably a better home-court advantage the Duquesne men have had in their history, and it was enjoyed three miles east, on another school's campus.

The University of Pittsburgh's Memorial (now Fitzgerald) Field House served as the home venue for Pitt basketball from its opening in 1951 through the 2001–02 season. After Duquesne basketball's home venue, the coincidentally named Duquesne Gardens, closed in 1956, Duquesne moved into the Field House as well, from the 1956–57 through 1963–64 seasons.

The Dukes' true home record over their first five seasons at the Field House was good if not outstanding, but a major highlight in program history occurred at the venue when Duquesne took a 79–74 overtime win from nationally ranked no. 2 St. Bonaventure on March 1, 1961. The result was so exciting for Duquesne that its president canceled the next day's classes.

If first impressions are important, so are last ones, and the final three seasons for the Dukes at the Field House were almost perfect, combining a 9-2 true home record in 1961–62, according to the Duquesne record book, with an 11-0 record in true home games from 1962–63 through 1963–64. Those records do not include games at the Pittsburgh Civic Arena, which opened in 1961 and welcomed the Dukes as an official home team (occasionally) beginning in 1963.

The Dukes headed full-time to the Civic Arena late in the 1963–64 season, but not before saying goodbye to the Field House as a home venue on February 15, 1964, by handily beating crosstown Carnegie Tech, 79–59. "Duquesne used a 40-minute full-court press and agitated the Tartans into numerous ball-handling mistakes," the *Pittsburgh Press* reported on the February 15 game.

Willie Somerset, an eventual Duquesne Sports Hall of Famer who earlier that season set a Civic Arena collegiate scoring record that will never be broken by tallying 47 points against Xavier in an 83–76 victory, led all players in the February 15 game with 22 points to move into fourth place on Duquesne's all-time scoring list behind All-Americans Dick Ricketts, Sihugo Green and Jim Tucker, respectively. Somerset would eventually pass Tucker and Green in career points and sits sixth in program history.

Somerset also scored 46 points in a 97–95 loss at St. Bonaventure earlier in the 1963–64 season to give him the two highest-scoring games in program history at that point, so the 22 he scored on February 15 seem almost paltry in comparison. Jules Borkowski led Carnegie Tech with 18 points.

Duquesne coach John "Red" Manning "seem[ed] bored with [the] Dukes' easy victory," the *Press* reported the next day.

But boring was probably a welcome sight for officials from both schools. "It was the last Duquesne-Tech game in the foreseeable future," according to the *Press*. "The two schools broke off relations last week after some fist swinging at the Civic Arena between the Duquesne freshmen and the Tech Jayvees.

"But yesterday's game was completely antiseptic, with both teams leaning over backwards to be on their best behavior."

Indeed, after forty-six official meetings between the two schools, according to the Duquesne record book, Carnegie Tech (now Carnegie Mellon University) and Duquesne have yet to resume their all-time series.

And with Duquesne basketball comfortably inside its sparkling UPMC Cooper Fieldhouse, the Dukes aren't likely to resume hosting games on Pitt's campus anytime soon, either.

Not that they didn't enjoy the results there.

38

THE GREATEST GAME THAT DIDN'T COUNT

Duquesne Basketball Defeats the Pittsburgh Pirates... Wait...Huh???

By David Finoli

A s I research information while writing books, I sometimes come across unexpected tidbits that pique my curiosity. I was doing research on the final men's basketball contest at the Fitzgerald Field House and was looking for the obligatory "this building was decrepit but boy did it have memories" article that always comes with the closing of a stadium or arena. Iconic Pittsburgh columnist Bob Smizik gave me what I was looking for. (I'll go into that more thoroughly in the next chapter.) But late in the column, he mentions the best game he ever saw at the Field House: an exhibition match in 1954 (actually late 1953) between Duquesne and an army base in Virginia by the name of Fort Belvoir. I was intrigued. More times than not, when I research these gems, I usually look at it, find out it wasn't as interesting as I thought and move on. In this case, Smizik was correct. It was not only a great game; it also caught my eye to the point that it became a chapter in this book.

The game took place at the Field House on December 15, 1953, with the gate receipts benefiting the Children's Fund, which, among other things, helped Children's Hospital. The Dukes at the time were 5-0, coming off a win the night before against Carnegie Tech and ranked third in the country. They eventually won their first twenty-two games, were ranked first in the nation for the only time in the program's existence and made it to the NIT finals (when the NIT was as important as the NCAA tournament) before

John (*left*) and Ed (*right*) O'Brien are twins who played for the Pittsburgh Pirates in the 1950s. Before they came to Pittsburgh, they were star basketball players at Seattle University, where John became the first player in the country to score 1,000 points in a career. The twins were on the Fort Belvoir squad that lost to Duquesne University, 72–70, at the Fitzgerald Field House. *Courtesy of the Pittsburgh Pirates.*

being upset by Holy Cross for a share of the national championship. For Fort Belvoir to play them so competitively, they had to have some good players. But the title of this chapter says they defeated the Pittsburgh Pirates, so what gives? Here is the unique twist to this contest.

The Korean War had just ended, so several athletes were still in the armed forces finishing their enlistment. Fort Belvoir had three players—Dick Groat, Johnny O'Brien and his brother Eddie O'Brien—who were college basketball greats. Groat was the NCAA Player of the Year in 1952 and a first team All-American. His no. 10 jersey for the Blue Devils was the first to be retired by the school. The O'Brien twins were stars at Seattle University, where Johnny became the first collegiate basketball player in the country to score 1,000 points in a career and Eddie starred on the team. In today's world, they each could have been NBA stars, but in the 1950s, the NBA was not the cash cow it eventually became. They all had incredible baseball talent, and since the money at that time was in Major League Baseball, they all became MLB players…for the Pittsburgh Pirates.

Dick Groat was one of the most memorable Pirates to ever play for the franchise, winning the National League MVP in 1960. Before choosing to play for the Bucs, he was a tremendous basketball player, being the first to have his number retired at Duke. In 1953, he was the star of a charity game at the Fitzgerald Field House, scoring 25 points as Duquesne defeated Groat's squad from Fort Belvoir, 72–70. *Courtesy of the Pittsburgh Pirates.*

On this evening, though, they represented their army base and did so magnificently. Groat led the way with 25 points, hitting shots from everywhere on the floor to the point that it amazed Duquesne star sophomore Si Green and his legendary coach Dudey Moore. Johnny O'Brien was second with 12 points.

The contest was an exciting back-and-forth game. It was a 1-point contest after each of the first three quarters. The Dukes had a 59–58 lead at the end of three and stretched it to 5 points early in the final period. Led by their three stars—Dick Ricketts (16 points), Jim Tucker (15) and Green (15)—as well as guard Lou Iezzi (15 points), Duquesne couldn't hold off Fort Belvoir, who tied the game at 70 with two minutes to play. With no time clock, Moore told his players to keep the ball until there were about ten seconds left, then get it to Green.

The team did just that. The visitors didn't press, so it was easy for Duquesne to keep the ball and run the clock down, as they instead chose to clog the lane to keep the Dukes from an easy layup. Finally, they got the ball to Si.

He played an incredibly athletic style of game at a time when basketball was played with many passes, station-to-station. When Green got the ball, he sped past a defense that couldn't keep up with him and hit the winning shot from the foul line for the 72–70 victory.

From all accounts, Smizik was right on the button. This was the most exciting game played at this facility that never counted. On this evening, the three Pirates had no answers for Si Green on the game's final play.

39

MAKING A STATEMENT

Pitt and WVU Play Their Last Backyard Brawl at the Fitzgerald Field House

By David Finoli

I t was tough picking the final memory in the section of the book for a building that still exists. Do we take another from the excellent yet disappointing run of Paul Evans in the late 1980s? How about from the year Ben Howland took this program to a level it hadn't seen since the days of Doc Carlson? Do we report on the Temple contest that took place on February 20, 1974, the day Pitt won its twenty-second in a row under Buzz Ridl in a season that ended in the Elite Eight? Those all would be excellent choices, especially the final one. Instead, the choice for the final chapter in this section is the final men's basketball game played at the Fitzgerald Field House, on March 3, 2002.

The game had many angles. After surprising the college basketball world with a trip to the Big East finals the year before, this Pitt team proved to be one of the best in the country. They finished ninth in the final AP poll and went on to win a school record twenty-nine games while finishing the year with a Sweet Sixteen appearance in the NCAA tournament. This game would also be the last Backyard Brawl contest at the Field House against their archrivals, the Mountaineers of West Virginia. It was a game the Panthers felt they needed to win to get a high enough seed in the tournament to be able to stay home and play their first two games at the Mellon Arena, which was hosting tourney games this season. The final angle that made this game the one to choose is that I found the obligatory column on how the old facility was trash yet had great memories and the new one would be an architectural marvel.

Iconic Pittsburgh columnist Bob Smizik (yes, I know I used the same description in the last chapter, but the man was iconic) said in a column written in the *Pittsburgh Post-Gazette* on February 27, 2002: "There were expansions, remodelings, refurbishings, and updatings. And when they were all done the one-time dump still looked like a dump. But it's been our dump for more than 50 years." He later went on to say, "But when Fitzgerald is rocking, as it has again this season, there's no better sports venue in town." There you have it, a dump with great memories.

Smizik was right. When the Fitzgerald Field House was full, as it was on this evening, with a capacity crowd of 6,798, there was no louder or more intimidating place to play in the city.

It was a celebratory evening against a team that usually gave them fits, but not on this night. This was a bad West Virginia team coming into the contest with a 1-14 conference mark. On this evening, they would lose their twentieth game of the season, which marked the first time the school ever lost twenty games. Despite that fact, 130 players came back to give the Fitzgerald a fitting send-off. They lined the sidelines to celebrate. Julius Page, who ended up with a game-high 23 points, said in an ESPN.com recap of the contest: "We were fired up with all of the old players there. I had to calm down because I was getting too fired up."

He calmed down a bit, but the Panthers took the momentum of the pregame celebration to the floor. They moved out to a 39–29 advantage before the Mountaineers came back to cut the deficit to five. After that, Pitt went on a 20–4 run in the second half to put the game away in a 92–65 rout.

The win helped the Panthers get a high seed in the NCAA tournament and their date in the Mellon Arena, where they defeated Central Connecticut State and California in the first two rounds. More importantly, the victory gave the Fitzgerald Field House a proper ending and memory for the many Pitt fans who had cheered on the Panthers in this "dump" over the more than five decades it was home to the men's basketball program.

IV

THE DUQUESNE GARDENS
(1890–1956)

Sihugo Green is among the top players to wear a Duquesne uniform. The school's only two-time consensus All-American, Green helped lead his team to not only two consecutive top-ten finishes but also the Dukes' lone national championship, in 1955. *Courtesy of Duquesne University Athletics.*

40

THE DUQUESNE GARDENS WAS FERTILE GROUND FOR SPORTS OF ALL SORTS

The History of the Duquesne Gardens

By Tom Rooney

Oakland was Pittsburgh's first "sports campus," with outdoor stadiums that were the home of baseball, pro football and big-time college football. In terms of indoor sports, Oakland was the location of an arena that hosted every imaginable sporting contest, including a startup in what would become the National Basketball Association and expansion in the National Hockey League. Add to that an array of other sports staged there, including tennis, and the city's only national title in college basketball. Even more notable, this venue hosted a great segment of Western Pennsylvania's illustrious boxing history. At one time, more than half of the reigning individual weight-class national champs hailed from the region. Indeed, in the first half of the 1900s, if it was a big-time sporting event, it was held in Oakland, a neighborhood in the eastern section of Pittsburgh dissected by Centre Avenue. Oakland was the center of all indoor spectator sports.

There were three Oakland venues, and they were built over a thirty-year period around the turn of the twentieth century. The outdoor state-of-the-art palaces, Forbes Field and Pitt Stadium, enjoyed red-hot success, hosting national champions almost right off the proverbial bat. The indoor arena, however, had much less of a hot start. Although, notably, the Duquesne Gardens was truly the result of a fire on ice.

The Duquesne Gardens was originally built in 1890 as a trolley barn housing some of the city's streetcars before it was converted to a sports arena following a fire at the Schenley Park Casino, which had served as the city's indoor sports arena before that. It ended up with an impressive history before being razed in 1956 to make room for apartment buildings. *Courtesy of the Pennsylvania Trolley Museum.*

Forbes Field opened midseason for the Pittsburgh Pirates in 1909 and, that same fall, hosted a hometown World Series champion. The Honus Wagner–led Bucs defeated the Ty Cobb–headlined Detroit Tigers in a maximum seven-game thriller of a series. Pitt Stadium was christened in 1925, and the football Panthers went 8-1 that campaign. The new stadium was credited as the home turf for five national champions in the next dozen years under the tutelage of legendary coach Jock Sutherland. These were great debuts for the new digs.

But the oldest of the three, the indoor arena known as "The Gardens," wasn't even constructed as a sports venue when it was built in 1890. The fact is, it was a repurposed streetcar barn that lasted only a few years in that deployment. The streetcars went out on a rail in 1897–98 after a fire incinerated the city's first indoor rink, the Schenley Casino. Unlike the exciting kickoffs of Forbes Field and Pitt Stadium, what transpired at the Duquesne Gardens was not the stuff of champions.

First, about that famous fire, from a man who is known as a streetcar conductor of trolley lore.

"An entrepreneur named Christopher Magee had built the Schenley Park Casino, one of the first artificial ice surfaces in North America," said retired Pennsylvania Trolley Museum archivist Edward Lybarger in an interview with the author. Lybarger held that post at the popular Washington, Pennsylvania tourist stop for twenty-five years. "Magee was also engaged in the trolley lines business, having owned Transverse Passenger Railway before rolling that up into a bigger network known as the Consolidated Traction Company. So when his very popular Casino rink burned to the ground December 17, 1896, he looked for a quick solution." Lybarger continued: "Seems one of the newer nearby trolley barns, which itself was only a few years old but soon to be rendered redundant by the railway's new Homewood Shops, appealed to him as a great project to convert."

On October 7, 1898, after a $300,000 renovation, the new Duquesne Gardens opened. The streetcar facility was sturdy, measuring 408 feet by 150 feet and made of solid brick with sandstone trimming. It had an ultimate capacity of 5,500 and was ideal as an arena. The first hockey game was held on January 24, 1899, when the Pittsburgh Athletic Club defeated Western University of Pennsylvania (later known as Pitt), 4–0.

Of all the sports hosted at the Gardens, hockey would have the longest legacy. But basketball was also a prime mover of patrons through the turnstiles. Duquesne University won the 1954–55 men's National Invitational Tournament at Madison Square Garden while playing its home dates at the Duquesne Gardens. The NIT was then on equal footing with the NCAA, and the two tournaments were often run on the same dates, so that a qualifying team had to pick one or the other. The Dukes were attracted to that other Gardens and chose to play in New York, bringing back to the "Bluff" the city's lone national college basketball championship.

"The N.I.T. championship game pitted the Dukes against Dayton for an unheard-of fourth time in the same season," says David Finoli, whose book *Kings of the Bluff* brilliantly captures the details of that championship. The Dukes were led by All-Americans Si Green and Dick Ricketts. "From their home court at Duquesne Gardens to the ultimate prize at the Madison Square Garden was quite a ride for the 'Red and Blue' from the Bluff," Finoli added.

Earlier than that 1955 event, in what is recognized as the 1946–47 National Basketball Association's inaugural season, a team named the Pittsburgh Ironmen played at the Duquesne Gardens. The NBA was originally called the BAA, the Basketball Association of America. The infant Ironmen franchise struggled to a sorry 15-45 record that produced poor attendance. It was "one (season) and done," and the NBA never returned to Pittsburgh, except for neutral-site games at the Gardens and later at the Civic Arena.

The 5,500-seat Duquesne Gardens held court from 1896 until 1956, when it became so dilapidated that it had to be razed. Promoters could no longer hang on for the hoped-for new arena. Patience for a promised new arena had run out, and plans had been kicked to the curb again and again. It would be a long five years before the new Civic Arena opened in 1961 on the downtown side of the Hill District separating Pittsburgh from Oakland.

The Duquesne Gardens may have been gone, but it was not forgotten, thanks to hockey, which became synonymous with its name. The venue served as a great foundation for what future generations of Pittsburghers would enjoy with the Pittsburgh Penguins, one of the most successful franchises in the modern history of the National Hockey League. The NHL Penguins and their older fans recognize the roots that the historians of the Gardens held in cold storage between arenas.

Not that hockey didn't have its slippery moments out there earlier in Oakland. Fans think of the Penguins when they think of the NHL. But there was another Pittsburgh team that claimed NHL big-league status. That franchise was built on an even earlier foundation.

"Pittsburgh had semi-professional hockey teams that had paid their players in the early 1900s," said Bob Grove, Pittsburgh's well-regarded and unofficial hockey historian. "There was a very successful West Penn Hockey League. And in 1925, the National Hockey League, in a pre-emptive move to stop Pittsburgh from becoming a building block of a new major league, awarded the city an expansion franchise."

That team was named the Pirates—also the original name of the Pittsburgh Steelers. The city was following a practice common in many markets: giving teams the same moniker as a popular existing team in the city. And the baseball Pirates were plenty good and very popular.

Those NHL Pirates tried to make a go of it at the Gardens for five seasons (1925–30), but poor attendance, made worse by the ensuing Great Depression, drove the franchise out of business.

But in the hallowed halls of the Hockey Hall of Fame in Toronto, those early teams are remembered for the famous players who skated for Pittsburgh. "Al Smith, Thomas Smith, Riley Hearn, Hod Stuart, Jimmy Gardner, Cyclone Taylor and Bruce Stewart all played in the West Penn League and they are Hall of Famers," said Grove. "And Roy Worters, Lionel Conacher, Mickey MacKay and Frank Frederickson are one time hockey Pirates you can find enshrined in Toronto," he added.

The Pittsburgh hockey Hornets arrived at the Duquesne Gardens in 1936 after relocating from Detroit as the American Hockey League's minor league affiliate of the Red Wings. They would win that league's Calder Cup championship in the 1951–52 campaign and then again in 1954–55. They were not able to successfully defend the title in 1955–56 and played their last game in the Duquesne Gardens on March 31, 1956. When the franchise was revived in 1961 with the opening of the Civic Arena, the Hornets would give way to the NHL Penguins in 1967, but not before winning a last Calder Cup in that last 1966–67 season.

The Hornets' final championship season leading up to the debut of the Penguins came with baggage for some. Newly hired Penguins general manager Jack Riley figured he had loaded up with veterans with a win-first philosophy. It backfired when the team suffered injuries to those vets and failed to make the playoffs the first two NHL seasons. "I'd have done it differently otherwise," Riley admitted. "I thought we had to win right away. The Hornets haunted me, they were a tough act to follow."

To Hornet fans—and those who had only reluctantly become Penguins fans—the early struggles of the Penguins led to chants of "Bring back the Hornets!," an indignity Riley suffered quietly from the press box. The Duquesne Gardens was long gone, but its longtime hockey tenant still lived in the loud complaints of Pittsburgh hockey fans: "Bring back the Hornets!"

41

THE NBA COMES TO PITTSBURGH...AND THEN DISAPPEARS

By David Finoli

There has always been a debate as to whether or not Pittsburgh could be a professional basketball town. While it has shown itself to be supportive of college basketball at times over the years, there hasn't been a consistent metric to tell whether it could support pro ball. At the professional level, the city showed potential for the way it supported the Pittsburgh Pipers toward the end of their championship run in 1968, but there have been more down moments in pro hoops, with a substandard minor league attempt, along with the poor showing in the stands with the Pittsburgh Condors. The city did have one chance to prove itself at the highest level of professional basketball, in 1946–47 with the Pittsburgh Ironmen, who played in a league called the Basketball Association of America (BAA). The BAA and its major competitor, the National Basketball League, merged in 1949 to form the National Basketball Association. The BAA is thus considered a precursor to the NBA and its records part of NBA history. So, in essence, the NBA had come to Pittsburgh, if only for a short time.

The team was owned by John W. Harris, a local entrepreneur who seemingly owned just about every sport that was performed indoors. He founded and owned the city's wildly successful American Hockey League team, the Pittsburgh Hornets. After inviting Olympic figure skating legend Sonja Henie to perform between periods of a Pittsburgh–Atlantic

City hockey playoff game at the Gardens, he came up with the idea for a show called the Ice Capades. When he got the opportunity to delve into professional basketball, he took advantage and started the Ironmen.

His first move was to hire as coach the first basketball player from Duquesne University to earn All-American status, Paul Birch. What he got in Birch was a man who closely resembled Bobby Knight. Unfortunately, Birch resembled Knight in terms of temper, not winning ability. According to his page on the Peach Basket Society website, Birch's son Richard described his temper as "Bobby Knight times 10." Fellow Duquesne alum Moe Becker, who played on the Ironmen, stated on the Temple Entertainment and Media website: "He used to be easy to get along with in Youngstown [where Birch coached him prior]; he turned into a monster in Pittsburgh."

There were reports that Birch used derogatory terms toward his players, threw a heavy wooden chair across the locker room in a fit of anger, made guard Press Maravich (Pete's father and former coach at LSU) stay in the shower after a loss and threatening to fine him $100 if he came out and other fits of rage in a frustrating season. His insistence on playing a zone defense, which slowed the game down, forced the league to implement a rule making that defense illegal. Needless to say, Paul Birch was not a popular figure.

Also irritated because he got a late start on recruiting players, Birch explained his temper in the book *The First Tip-Off* by Charlie Rosen: "That's something coaches do. There's nothing exceptional about it. My coaches did the same thing when I played. It's just a way to show the players that you're really pissed." It may have been what Birch intended, but there was a difference between what he did to his players and what his former coach, Chick Davies at Duquesne, who was an advisor on the Ironmen, did. Davies's players actually knew that he cared for them. Birch's players seemingly did not.

After a loss to St. Louis to open the season, Pittsburgh hosted Red Auerbach and the Washington Capitals in the home opener at the Duquesne Gardens. A little over three thousand people showed up at the arena that Birch said "had the worst court in the league. It wasn't compact, and when the underlying ice started to melt, the water seeped through the spaces between the floorboards."

They lost that game, 71–56, and then dropped to 1-4 before Colby Gunther was signed. Gunther went on to lead the team with 14.1 points per game, but he seemingly did more to hurt the Ironmen than help them. While they were built on an unselfish passing offense, Gunther had the philosophy of shoot first and ask questions later. He was very selfish, according to those who played with him.

Pittsburgh kept losing, and when they met the Boston Celtics on the final game of the season at the Gardens, only 770 fans showed up to see them blown out. They finished 15-45, in last place. Birch was soon fired. Following a season in which Harris lost $200,000 and averaged only 1,363 fans at the Gardens, the owner decided to keep the team but be inactive for the 1947–48 campaign while he reorganized. They never took the court again.

When Nate Silver rated every professional basketball team on his website FiveThirtyEight, the 1946–47 Pittsburgh Ironmen finished dead last. It was a fitting legacy for Pittsburgh's only NBA squad, arguably the most troubled franchise in the history of the league.

42

A BUSY DAY IN THE 'BURGH

The Pirates Open Forbes Field, Then Fans Walk the Short Distance to the Duquesne Gardens to See Heavyweight Champion Jack Johnson Take on Tony Ross

By Douglas Cavanaugh and David Finoli

In the many decades that these four magnificent facilities stood only one-quarter of a mile from one another, no day better illustrates what an advantage it was for Steel City sports fans than June 30, 1909. It was arguably the most significant day in the history of sports in western Pennsylvania.

The day started out showcasing the first all-steel-and-concrete stadium built in the National League, Forbes Field. For most of the first decade of the twentieth century, the Pirates fielded one of the best teams in the game. In fact, between 1901 and 1903, they had the first dynasty in professional sports in the twentieth century. They were led by Hall of Famers Honus Wagner and Fred Clarke, who put up gaudy numbers despite the fact that they had to play in the flood-infested confines of Exposition Park.

Built on the shores of where the three rivers meet in Pittsburgh (the exact spot where Three Rivers Stadium stood), Exposition Park did not have the modern amenities to keep water from the field of play when the river levels expanded. As the first decade was coming to an end, Pirate Hall-of-Fame owner Barney Dreyfuss was becoming irritated with the situation and finally deemed it necessary to move to drier lands. He found such a place in the Oakland section of Pittsburgh. It took four months to build what was hailed

Probably the best example of how having so many facilities so close together was great for Pittsburgh sports fans occurred on June 30, 1909. After seeing the opening of Forbes Field, fans made the short walk to the Duquesne Gardens, where heavyweight champion Jack Johnson (*pictured*) fought Tony Ross. *Courtesy of Cornell University Digital Library.*

as an architectural masterpiece, and on June 30, 1909, it opened its doors for the first time.

It was a magnificent day, with clear skies and temperatures in the low eighties as 30,338 patrons crammed into a facility that was supposed to hold only 25,000. It was an exciting game that the Chicago Cubs won, 3–2, after scoring 2 runs in the eighth, one on a dropped throw to the plate by catcher George Gibson and another when Gibson chose to go to first on a bunt by the Cubs' Harry Steinfeldt instead of trying to tag out Jimmy Sheckard, who was coming home on the play.

Despite the disappointment on that day, the Bucs went on to win their fourth National League pennant in 1909 and brought a World Series to Forbes Field in its inaugural season. There was also other excitement for sports fans in Pittsburgh to help them get over the loss to Chicago. The heavyweight champion of the world, Jack Johnson, was in the Steel City for a fight that evening, and those going to both events had just a short walk to make.

The exciting sports day continued into the night for the fans who streamed out of Forbes Field, crossed the street and made their way to the Duquesne Gardens to watch newly crowned champion Jack Johnson, the first African American titlist in division history, swap punches with local favorite Tony Ross, the "Italian Bearcat."

The National Athletic Club had recently been formed by Red Mason and Jimmy Dime, the two most influential boxing men in Pittsburgh. (Mason was a giant in local sports and could accurately be described as the Art Rooney of his day, though he was much more impulsive and belligerent than the calm, diplomatic Rooney.) The Duquesne Gardens was the headquarters of the National AC, the formation of which catapulted the Steel City to a new level of importance and credibility on the national boxing scene. Dime knew that having a heavyweight king contesting there would boost Pittsburgh boxing to even loftier heights, so he seized the opportunity of Johnson appearing by offering the "Galveston Giant" a huge sum of money to fight at the Gardens to start the summer season.

Johnson had recently returned to America after spending a long time overseas chasing the title, then held by the diminutive Canadian Tommy Burns. Jack finally got his chance in Sydney, Australia, on December 26, 1908, winning the crown in round fourteen. When Johnson returned to the United States five months later, he fought another opponent whom he outweighed by a considerable amount, causing sportswriters to accuse him of "picking on" smaller men and being afraid to take on real challenges.

Johnson was incensed by the accusation, having spent years seeking out and fighting any and every heavyweight who would sign on the dotted line. One of the big digs against him was that he was a conservative fighter, more concerned with defense and protecting his handsome face than actually digging in and making a fight of it. So, when Jimmy Dime presented him with the opportunity to battle Tony Ross, who was in fact larger than the heavyweight champ, Jack grabbed it with both hands and promised to make the American press eat its words.

He did exactly as he said he would, taking a much more aggressive approach to Ross than he had in previous bouts. He battered, bloodied and floored the brave Italian, scoring a lopsided six-round newspaper decision to end what was truly a memorable day in the city.

43

A PITTSBURGH FIGHT EXTRAVAGANZA

The Conn-Zivic Fight

By Douglas Cavanaugh

Two Pittsburgh icons who represented different aspects of a multifaceted American city were Billy Conn and Fritzie Zivic.

Conn was movie-star handsome, smiling and energetic—perfect qualities to capture the fancy of the media and the casual sports fan. Zivic was rugged, wryly sneering and (comparatively) reserved—qualities that endeared him to the tough, working-class man and hardcore sports fan. One was Irish, the other Croatian. One was from East Liberty, the other from Lawrenceville. One was a young upstart with thirty-six fights under his belt. The other was a grizzled veteran of sixty-eight ring wars. One was cocky, and the other was confident.

Pittsburgh could hardly wait for this donnybrook when the two men signed to fight in late 1936 at the Duquesne Gardens.

The local press naturally hyped this as a "grudge match," as if Conn and Zivic were bitter enemies. But in truth the only hostility was that between their managers, Johnny Ray for Conn and Luke Carney for Zivic. Billy and Fritz were in fact friends when Carney saw an opportunity for his fighter and threw out challenges to Pittsburgh's two top middleweights, Conn and Teddy Yarosz. The resulting negotiations created bitterness between the managers, which the newspapers reported had trickled down onto the fighters.

Many in the press felt that Ray was rushing young Billy, matching him against tough opposition so early in his career. Their protests hit a fever pitch when Ray signed him to fight wily veteran Zivic, a dangerous contender with far more experience and a pronounced mean streak in the ring. What did Conn have to gain by fighting a welterweight like Fritzie? As Johnny Ray saw it, a lot. For one, Billy was a tough and skillful boxer in his own right and would have significant advantages in weight, height and reach. Plus, these were two of the biggest names in local sports, both with large followings. That would sell tickets and pack the Duquesne Gardens. He saw it as a win-win.

Ray guessed correctly. The venue was packed on the night of December 28, the crowd shrieking themselves hoarse at the shifts in momentum. As expected, the favored Zivic went right after Conn, getting past his reach and instigating a rugged inside attack to take the initial rounds. Realizing that the clever Croat was too skilled to battle close, Billy shifted gears and used his long left jab and outside game to turn the tide in his favor. In the final stanzas, it was anyone's fight. Both men gave all they could until the bell ending the tenth and final round.

Conn was awarded a razor-thin unanimous decision. Zivic had his boosters, but everyone left the Garden that night fully satisfied with the fight they had witnessed. There was no loser. But Billy later commented: "He [Zivic] put a face on me. My mother didn't recognize me for five days."

Both went on to become world champions soon after and invaded the New York fight scene and became big draws in the Big Apple. This brought them closer together as friends. They supported each other at all times, one almost always in the audience when the other was fighting.

They connected on the level of humor as well, each good for the clever comment or story when the press asked. Zivic once relayed an experience that underscored the East Liberty Irish lad's humor, which had few boundaries and almost no discretion, even during one of the most stressful, pressure-packed nights of Fritzie's career:

"I get a great kick out of him [Conn]," he said. "The night I fought Henry Armstrong the second time, he came into my dressing room before the fight and says to me:

"'Come here, you.'

"And then he says, 'Listen. I got thirty-five bucks in my pocket and I just bet nine Cs on you. If you don't win, stay in that ring, because if you come out I will cut your heart out.'

"And then when we are in the ring and Conn gets introduced and he comes to my corner, everybody thinks he is wishing me luck. But he bends down and says:

"'Remember. Nine Cs. That's blood money, Zivic.'"

44

SUGAR AND SPICE

The Great Sugar Ray Robinson Takes on Sammy Angott

By Douglas Cavanaugh

Ray (Sugar) Robinson wins with the same monotonous regularity as the Democrats in Mississippi, so it's understandable why there'll be no wagering against him at the Gardens tomorrow night.
—Pittsburgh Press

The fluid boxing and explosive punches of the speedy Sugar Ray Robinson were too much of an obstacle for just about every fighter of his era to overcome. Sugar Ray was darn near unbeatable in those years and was knocking out almost everybody. But in Sammy Angott he found a stubborn foe who not only stood up to his punishment but also gave a fair share of it in return. Sammy even had the audacity to taunt Robinson late in a bout by laughing and telling him to "come on and fight."

Like fellow Pittsburgher Fritzie Zivic, Angott always put up a good fight against the "Sugar Man" and did his hometown proud. Their first bout took place in Philadelphia during the summer of 1941, when Robinson was a mere lightweight with a 20-0 record. Sammy was an eighty-fight veteran and had already been in there with several champions and challengers. But experience and strength were the only advantages Angott had, and Ray was able to use his superior height, reach, skill and power to outduel "The Clutch" and take the ten-round decision.

It was essentially Robinson's coming-out party, much like the victory over Charley Burley was Ezzard Charles's coming-out event. Both wins gave notice to the boxing world that a new threat had arrived. Sugar Ray proved to everyone that he was not some nervous upstart kid who would wilt under the pressure of a big, important bout. To do as well as he did against a tough and seasoned veteran like Sammy was a revelation to everyone. Everything they said about him was true. The speed, the power, the grace, the talent—it was all there in abundance.

The two met a year later at Madison Square Garden in New York. By this time, Robinson was beginning to grow into his prime welterweight size and had several pounds on Angott, not to mention an imposing 32-0 (25 KOs) record. It featured Sammy charging in and throwing hard to the head and body, keeping things close and perhaps even getting the better of the first five rounds. But Robinson's superior firepower took its toll, and "The Clutch" slowed from the sixth round on as bomb after whiplash bomb caromed off his granite chin. As always, Angott took it and kept boring in on his lanky foe, but he ultimately fell short, losing another ten-rounder.

The third bout took place at the Duquesne Gardens on March 4, 1946. Ray was now a veteran and in his absolute prime, considered to be the deadliest fighter this side of Joe Louis. He sported an incredible 62-1-1 record (his one loss, to Jake LaMotta, avenged threefold) and was, like Angott, a huge draw in Pittsburgh. The fighters broke all Duquesne Gardens records that night, the crowd going wild as they tore into one another. Ray once again won a unanimous decision in ten rounds.

The record shows that Robinson floored Sammy several times and won their series convincingly. But a deeper investigation reveals that Angott, with his awkward style, made Ray work for it every minute of every round. The Italian forced matters all the time, crouching, rolling, weaving, wrestling and mauling as he battered Ray's body with blows, even forcing him to the ropes on several occasions. But the younger, fresher and more talented Robinson ultimately had too much skill and firepower to be denied.

Ray was the better man in their three-bout series. But he came away with a large measure of respect for the mighty-muscled little mauler—one of the few fighters in the world who could survive Robinson's thunder and come back swinging. Angott was nobody's "punk" or stepping-stone, which Robinson attested to in the press: "Sammy is a tough man to fight…the old fellow is just too smart. He's all arms, and his unorthodox style makes him hard to hit."

That was high praise from the man many consider to be the greatest ever to the man many forget was one of the toughest ever.

45

SONJA HENIE COMES TO PITTSBURGH

The Ice Capades Are Born at the Gardens

By David Finoli

I t was a fairly one-sided affair for the Pittsburgh Yellow Jackets on March 31, 1936, at the Duquesne Gardens. They were facing the Atlantic City Seagulls in the round robin Eastern Amateur Hockey League playoffs for the vaunted Hershey Cup. Frank Brimsek was stellar in goal for the Jackets, while Red Sherwood had a hat trick in the 9–0 drubbing by Pittsburgh over the Seagulls. The win gave the Yellow Jackets a second-place finish in the playoffs. The Baltimore Orioles clinched the Hershey Cup. As thrilling as it must have been for the capacity crowd of six thousand at the Gardens, the story of the game itself was a very small part of writer Fred Landucci's piece in the *Pittsburgh Press* the next day. The main part of the evening was what took place before the game. The night saw a performance by one of the greatest figure skaters who ever took to the ice. It was the evening Sonja Henie came to Pittsburgh.

In the 1920s, the Pittsburgh Yellow Jackets had been the premier amateur team in the country, winning two national championships, in 1924 and 1925, before morphing into the Pittsburgh Pirates of the NHL (more on that in the next chapter). After the Pirates moved to Philadelphia, the Jackets reemerged in 1930. By 1933, the man who would own just about every indoor professional team in Pittsburgh, John Harris, had taken control of them. Harris knew entertainment and thought that figure skating was an enterprise that could make some money. Sonja Henie was a superstar on the skating circuit, winning ten consecutive world championships and three

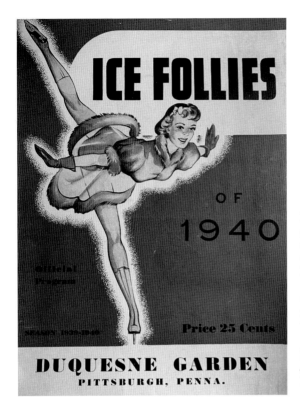

Pictured here is a program from the Ice Follies, which came to the Duquesne Gardens in 1940. The Ice Follies was the rival to the Ice Capades, founded by Hornet owner John Harris that year from an idea he came up with in 1936, when he invited Sonja Henie to skate between periods of a Pittsburgh Yellow Jackets playoff game. It was a performance that fans loved. *Courtesy of David Finoli.*

Olympic gold medals (1928, 1932 and 1936). She wanted to be a movie star. Eventually, the woman they called the "Ice Queen of Norway" would do just that. Henie was on a tour of the United States to show her immense talent and promote her upcoming film debut. Harris wanted to see if his inclinations were correct. They were.

The capacity crowd was not on hand to see a meaningless playoff game in which the best the home team could do was finish second. They were there to see Sonja. In fact, 1,500 fans had to be turned away. Landucci described the performance: "Never have Pittsburghers seen such fancy, figure and interpretive skating as the little Norwegian girl showed them. She made three appearances and was wildly acclaimed on each. Each ovation was greater than the preceding and last, when she skated off the ice, was a tremendous tribute to a great artist."

Henie skated before the game and then between each period. Landucci claimed that the hockey game "was merely incidental to the major attraction."

The crowd was ecstatic, demanding encores each time she ended her performance. Harris was more than convinced at this point of the monetary opportunities in figure skating. That night in Pittsburgh's Duquesne Gardens, unbeknownst to the large throng, the Ice Capades was born. Four years later, the Arena Managers Association—leaders of some of the biggest arenas in the country, including the Boston Gardens, the Buffalo Memorial Auditorium, the Cleveland Arena, the Hershey Sports Arena, the New Haven Arena, the Philadelphia Arena, the Rhode Island Auditorium and the Springfield Auditorium—joined Harris in Hershey, Pennsylvania, to iron out the particulars. The Ice Capades became a reality. It debuted on June 16, 1940, at the New Orleans Municipal Auditorium and became a hit. Harris became its president and remained so until 1964, when he sold the show to a company by the name of Metromedia.

While Henie's performance is still remembered for the beginning of the legendary show, few remember Red Sherwood's big evening. That's what happens when a hockey game turns "incidental" to the beginning of a legendary gate attraction.

46

A BLACK AND GOLD LOVEFEST

The Yellow Jackets Morph into the Pirates

By David Finoli

Many fans of Pittsburgh sports believe that the black-and-gold color combinations they hold so dear for their pro teams began with the Pirates and the Steelers. But that isn't the case. The baseball Pirates sported red-and-blue uniforms until 1948. The Steelers (then also nicknamed the Pirates) did precede the Bucs, choosing the color combination when they entered the NFL in 1933, but they also weren't the first. The honor goes to the second professional team to be named the Pirates, the city's first entry in the NHL. They donned the colors at the Duquesne Gardens in 1925 after they morphed from the town's highly successful amateur club, the Yellow Jackets, another resident of the Gardens. The Yellow Jackets also wore the famed colors. In fact, if the Pirates had chosen other colors to represent their team, perhaps the Penguins wouldn't have been allowed to become the third and final black-and-gold team in the Steel City. But we will get to that later.

The Yellow Jackets were founded by a man named Roy Schooley, a former City of Pittsburgh treasurer who also managed the Duquesne Gardens and later was a key part of starting the USA Hockey program (in Pittsburgh) that went on to win silver at the 1920 Summer Olympics in Antwerp. They played in the United States Amateur Hockey Association beginning in 1920 and, within four years, had become the greatest amateur team in the country.

Led by the great Lionel Conacher (arguably the premier player of the era), Hib Milks, Duke McCurry, Harold Cotton, Harrold Darragh and goalies Roy Worters and Frank Brimsek, the team finished the 1924 campaign with a 15-5 mark before defeating the Boston Athletic Association for their first league title.

Their coach, Dick Carroll, who captured the 1918 Stanley Cup while heading the Toronto Arenas, found it easy to recruit top players. According to Conacher, quoted in the book *Pittsburgh's Greatest Teams*: "This here's a real hockey town for sure. The boys up north think they're in heaven after they get here." Whether they confused it for heaven, Iowa or Pittsburgh, the Yellow Jackets were the city's first hockey dynasty when they completed a 25-11-5 season a year later while beating another local team, the Fort Pitt Hornets, at the Gardens to win their second consecutive title.

They were wildly popular in the city, and while they would return to the Gardens in 1930, staying until the Pittsburgh Hornets came to town, Schooley sold them to attorney James Callahan after their second title. He renamed them the Pirates and took them to the NHL as an expansion team in 1926.

It was at this time that the Pirates became the first professional team in the city to wear the esteemed black and gold. They stayed five years in the NHL before moving across the state in 1930–31 to become the Philadelphia Quakers. They had two decent seasons in the Steel City, becoming the first NHL Pittsburgh club to advance to the Final Four in the Stanley Cup playoffs (1925–26), then losing in the quarterfinals two years later. They also had three disastrous campaigns, the worst being their final season (1929–30), when they accumulated just 13 points in a 5-36-3 finale in the 'Burgh.

While their time in Pittsburgh was short, the team was known for two things. Hockey at the time was played by five players for the entire game for the most part, until Pirate coach Odie Cleghorn changed that with a strategy that took advantage of Pittsburgh's depth. Cleghorn was the first coach to use multiple lines in a game. He'd use his top line for the first half of the period, his second line for eight minutes and then insert the top line to finish the frame. It was revolutionary at the time and a major reason the team went to the semifinals.

The second thing they were known for was the black-and-gold uniforms. (Truth be told, in season four they switched to a gold-and-blue combination before reverting to black and gold in their final campaign.) It wasn't important at the time, but it gained relevance fifty years later, in 1980, when the Penguins wanted to join the Pirates and Steelers and make all of the professional Pittsburgh teams black-and-gold brothers. The Boston Bruins objected to the color change, claiming that they should be the only ones allowed to wear the color scheme. It was decided that since the Pirates were actually the first to wear the color combination, the Pens could continue the tradition of their predecessors and also don the colors. A black-and-gold tradition was now complete in Pittsburgh, thanks to the fact that two teams wore the colors on the ice of the Duquesne Gardens.

47

CHICK DAVIES OR DUDEY MOORE

Who Was the Greatest Basketball Coach at the Duquesne Gardens?

By David Finoli

So much local sports history happened at the Duquesne Gardens that to try to point out a single best moment is difficult. Determing the most successful team that called the Gardens home is an easier venture. Duquesne Dukes basketball was among the best college programs in the nation while they played at the Gardens, winning their lone national championship in the 1955 National Invitation Tournament. Among the main reasons for its success were the two men who ran the team between 1924 and 1958. Charles "Chick" Davies had a 314-106 mark in his career, and Donald "Dudey" Moore, a surprise choice to take over the program after Davies retired in 1948, went 191-70 in ten seasons. Moore also led the team to its national title before heading to LaSalle. These two men could be classified as 1A and 1B as far as the best coaches to grace the sidelines at the Duquesne Gardens. But who was the best?

Chick was certainly a legend in Duquesne circles and is considered the father of men's basketball at the school. He was hired by the administration in 1925 without a high school degree for $300 a year. He eventually not only got his diploma but also earned bachelor's and master's degrees on the Bluff.

Davies was considered a strict disciplinarian who put the school on the college basketball map. In his twenty-three years at Duquesne, he coached the 1940 team to the NIT finals and the program's only Final Four appearance in the NCAA tournament. It was the first time (along

Pictured in the Duquesne Gardens program from the 1948–49 season is head coach Donald "Dudey" Moore. Dudey was not the program's first choice, as more prominent Duquesne alums Moe Becker and Paul Birch were rumored to have been in consideration for the job. But he turned out to be the best choice. His impressive defensive philosophy helped lead the Dukes to much success and was featured in *Sports Illustrated* in 1958. *Courtesy of Duquesne University Athletics.*

with Colorado) that a team was invited to both major collegiate tourneys in the same season. His club, called the "Iron Dukes" between 1935 and 1937, went an impressive 48-3.

Overall, Chick, who recruited the great Chuck Cooper to the school, retired with a .749 winning percentage. At the time of his death in 1985, his winning percentage was still the twelfth-best mark all-time. As of 2022, it is the twenty-fifth best. These are impressive marks, but are they better than his successor's?

Dudey Moore wasn't necessarily the first choice of the school administration to replace Davies, having only high school coaching experience on his résumé. Rumors in the paper had the job being offered to two former Duquesne All-Americans, Moe Becker and Paul Birch, before Moore was surprisingly extended the offer.

While offense was the priority of most coaches in the era, Moore's defensive philosophy became his calling card, and it took the program to the next level, a position that the Dukes and North Carolinas of the world enjoy today. Moore thought that the stance was the most important part of a defender's play. He wanted the weight to be evenly distrusted on the balls of the feet, the body bent at the waist and the knees in a flexible, aggressive position. This stance allowed the defender to be in the best possible position to steal the ball. Moore's defensive philosophy helped spur the Dukes to their best era. The team achieved the program's first and only no. 1 ranking in the Associated Press poll in 1954 and finished in the NIT Final Four three consecutive seasons before leading Duquesne to their lone national championship in the 1955 NIT.

Pictured here is Duquesne University coach Donald "Dudey" Moore. He is considered one of the two greatest coaches in the program's history, along with his predecessor, Chick Davies. Moore finished his career on the Bluff with a 191-70 mark, leading the team to their lone national championship in 1955. *Courtesy of Duquesne University Athletics.*

The guard on the 1955 national championship squad, Mickey Winograd, described the coach this way: "Dudey was a great pregame coach. Every move was calculated." His final record with the Dukes was 191-70 for a .732 winning percentage.

Choosing between Moore and Davies is tough. The calculating Moore had strong recruiting skills, bringing such greats as Jim Tucker, Dick Ricketts and Sihugo Green to the Bluff. And his unique defensive philosophy and the fact that he completed the job of bringing a national championship to Pittsburgh gives him the nod over his disciplined predecessor as the greatest basketball coach at the Duquesne Gardens.

48

THE CITY OF CHAMPIONS

1955 at the Duquesne Gardens

By David Finoli

Much has been made of Pittsburgh being called the "City of Champions" over the years. In fact, it has become a common nickname when referring to the Steel City, which is Pittsburgh's other famous nickname. Of course, the champions moniker was used to celebrate the year 1979, when the Pirates and Steelers both won league championships in the same season, and the 2008–9 campaign, when the Penguins and Steelers both held titles at the same time. As memorable as those two years are, it wasn't the first time the city pulled off the impressive feat of winning two championships in a year. In 1967–68, the Hornets and the Pipers brought titles to the Civic Arena. And then there was the first time it happened, a year in which the Bucs finished the season in last place at 60-94 and the Steelers were a miserable 4-8. It was 1955, and the sports success Pittsburgh was enjoying was occurring at the Duquesne Gardens. It was the year that the Hornets and Duquesne University's men's basketball team both won championships, giving the city its first season as City of Champions.

The Dukes were one of the most celebrated basketball programs entering the 1954–55 campaign. The problem was, they were also considered the Buffalo Bills of their time, especially in the Dudey Moore era. They finished fourth in the NIT in 1950. (The NIT was considered as important as the NCAA tournament at the time.) And they finished fourth in 1952, third in 1953 and a runner-up in 1954 after an upset loss to Holy Cross in the finals.

In the program's defining moment, coach Dudey Moore gets carried off the floor after defeating Dayton in the 1955 National Invitation Tournament finals. Coupled with the Hornets' victory in the Calder Cup finals, it gave Pittsburgh its first year with a "City of Champions" designation. *Courtesy of Duquesne University Athletics.*

Each year, they were talented enough to win a national championship. But, like the Bills, each year, they fell short.

In 1955, they had a talented team that was not as deep or as good as the previous season. While they had several good players, such as Dave Ricketts and Mickey Winograd, the team was basically a two-headed monster with arguably the two greatest players in the program's history leading the way: Dick Ricketts and Sihugo Green. Even though depth was an issue, the team found a way to win. When Ricketts and Green were healthy, the Dukes were almost unbeatable, losing only one game when these two players were healthy at the same time.

The team battled through a 19-4 regular season while thrilling people at the Duquesne Gardens. Duquesne accepted another bid to the NIT, choosing it over an NCAA bid. They pushed their way to the finals, where they finally got over their runner-up reputation by beating Dayton, 70–58 in the finals. Ricketts and Green combined for 56 of the 70 points, including all 35 in the first half. It was the Dukes' first and, to date, only national championship

As the Dukes were playing through their memorable championship campaign, the local hockey team, the Pittsburgh Hornets, were having a solid if unspectacular season. They began the year by dropping their black-and-gold uniforms for their more traditional red-and-white ones, which they had worn earlier in their existence.

Led by new coach Howie Meeker and scoring leaders Willie Marshall and Earl Balfour, the Hornets were struggling midway with a record slightly over .500 (13-12-8). But 1955 was a parity season in the American Hockey League (AHL), and no team stood out. They played better in the second half and won the regular-season crown with a 31-25-8 mark.

In the Calder Cup playoffs, Jerry Foley scored an overtime goal in game four against the Springfield Indians to win the semifinal series three games to one. The Hornets faced the Buffalo Bisons in the finals.

The Hornets shot out to a three-games-to-one-lead and had a chance to win their second Calder Cup in franchise history at the Duquesne Gardens. Unfortunately, they lost the game, 5–4, and had to travel to Buffalo for game six. Marshall, who was named the playoff MVP with 9 goals and 16 points, scored an empty-net goal after the Bisons cut a 3–0 Pittsburgh lead going into the final period to 3–2. The Hornets won the Calder Cup, four games to two.

It was an amazing month for Pittsburgh sports fans. The stench of Pirate baseball and Steeler football was wiped away with these two amazing victories, wins that allowed the town to be called City of Champions for the very first time.

49

ALL SIGNS POINT TO THE END

The 1956 AHL All-Star Game

By David Finoli

It was supposed to be a day of celebration. The defending Calder Cup champion Pittsburgh Hornets took on the American Hockey League (AHL) All-Star team at the Duquesne Gardens in the 1956 AHL All-Star Game. What it became was a rumorfest. The supposed end of the Hornet franchise was being touted, despite vehement denials by Pittsburgh management. While the rumors being bandied about weren't true, it was soon announced that the Duquesne Gardens would become rubble within the next few months and the Hornets would be dismantled and put away in the closet—for five long years, it turned out. The day of celebration was certainly taking a back seat on this January day.

Beginning with the All-Star Game the year before, it became the new tradition that the defending AHL champions would be the home team against a squad of all-stars from the remaining teams in the league. (It was a short tradition, ending on December 10, 1959, when Hershey defeated the AHL stars, 8–3. It was the last All-Star Game in the league until 1995.) The game had taken a back seat to rumors that the Hornets were to be moved to Cincinnati for the 1956–57 campaign, despite the fact that members of Hornet management and league officials denied the rumors. The story came from a Cincinnati sportswriter who claimed that the Cincinnati Mohawks of the International League would reenter the AHL, giving the city a franchise for the first time since 1950–51, when the Mohawks left. While the story ended up being false, soon after the game ended, other factors came to light that would not be good news for the popular Hornet franchise.

A disappointing crowd of 2,032 fans showed up to the affair to see what turned out to be an exciting contest. Throughout most of the game, the Hornets enjoyed a distinct advantage, outshooting the AHL All-Stars 53-33. Pittsburgh opened the scoring when Joe Klusky beat Springfield's Don Simmons at 9:49 of the first period to give the Hornets a 1–0 lead.

The visitors took over at that point, scoring 3 unanswered goals to move on top of the Hornets, 3–1, before center Bob Hassard netted a goal with seventeen seconds left in the second period to cut the All-Stars' lead to 3–2. After Klusky tied the game early in the third with his second goal of the game, Buffalo's Ken Wharram restored the visitors' 1-goal advantage midway through the final period of regulation.

Pictured here is the 1952–53 jersey of the Pittsburgh Hornets. This jersey is in the black-and-gold tradition that Pittsburgh teams have worn proudly over the years. The Hornets would switch back to their more traditional red-and-white jerseys in 1954. *Courtesy of David Finoli.*

With time running out, defenseman Frank Mathers gathered the puck for Pittsburgh in his own end and rifled a pass to the team's leading scorer, Willie Marshall, who finished the year with 45 goals and 97 points in only 58 games. Marshall swept by a defenseman and put the puck behind Hershey goalie Johnny Henderson to tie it with only 1:05 remaining in regulation. The two teams played one ten-minute overtime period. Despite several scoring chances that were put aside by Henderson and Hornet goalie Gil Mayer, the game ended in a 4–4 tie.

It was a great contest and season for Pittsburgh, who finished in second place with a 43-17-4 mark before losing to the Cleveland Barons three games to one in the semifinals, including a 6–4 game two loss that would turn out to be the final game for the Hornets in the Duquesne Gardens.

It wasn't the fact that Pittsburgh was moving its franchise to Cincinnati that made the contest the final one at the Gardens. It was not. Rather, it was the fact that the Hornets were informed on February 16 that the building they played in was to be razed on April 30 and the proposed new facility, which eventually turned out to be the Civic Arena, would not be ready until 1958 at the earliest. (It was completed in 1961.) This left the Hornets without a place to play.

The eventual decision by the AHL and team management was to suspend the franchise until it had a suitable place to play. That, of course, took five long years, until they brought the team back, when the Civic Arena finally opened in 1961. While they would win a third Calder Cup title in 1967 before giving way to the Pittsburgh Penguins, the Hornets' long, successful run at the Duquesne Gardens was over, as all signs at the 1956 All-Star Game seemed to point to this inevitable end.

50

INDOOR TENNIS BEGINS IN PITTSBURGH EARLIER THAN YOU THINK

The Fred Perry and Ellsworth Vines Show Comes to the Gardens

By David Finoli

The general consensus among Pittsburgh sports fans is that indoor tennis was a phenomenon that began in Pittsburgh in the mid-1970s, when the Triangles came to town to compete in a new venture called World Team Tennis (WTT). While the Triangles were popular and captured the 1976 WTT championship, it wasn't the beginning of indoor tennis in the city. The beginning was almost seventy years earlier, in 1937, when newly anointed professionals Fred Perry and Ellsworth Vines came to the Duquesne Gardens as part of a seventy-match head-to-head tour.

In the 1930s, you were not permitted to play in any of the major tennis tournaments unless you were an amateur. After capturing one Wimbledon and two U.S. Open titles, Vines announced that he was becoming a pro in 1934. While it meant no more opportunities to win major tennis tournaments, it opened up new financial opportunities for him. Vines would have shots at winning professional tournaments for sure, but head-to-head exhibitions seemed to be where the money was, and that's what brought Perry and Vines together.

Perry, who won eight majors in his amateur career, including a career grand slam, was one of the greatest players England had ever produced. He wasn't a fan of the Lawn Tennis Club of Great Britain's poor attitude toward the lower classes, so he decided to turn pro and come to the United States, where he became a citizen in 1939.

As the story goes, after Perry decided to turn pro, he called Vines. According to a quote in a *Los Angeles Times* article by Thomas Bonk of December 11, 1990, Perry said: "I remember I told him it was Fred. He said 'are you crazy? It's 4 AM' and I said 'Do you want to make some money?' And Elly said 'Well that's different'." After that conversation, a forty-city, seventy-match tour was set up. It included a January date at the Duquesne Gardens.

Indoor courts in the 1930s were not as elaborate as they became later in the twentieth century. It was a wood court with a canvas stretched over the top. The court was taken apart at the end of a match and loaded onto a truck that was headed to the next city.

Pittsburgh was the fourth stop on the tour, which saw Perry capture the first three matches. The tour drew over 35,000 people, including a record at Madison Square Garden, where over 18,000 people were on hand. A capacity crowd at the Duquesne Gardens attended the match on this evening, but the fans who were there weren't exactly sure what they'd see out of Vines. He had come down with the flu and spent five days in a Chicago hospital trying to recover. Perry was happy his opponent seemed in better shape, saying in a *Pittsburgh Post-Gazette* article the day before the match: "I am glad that Vines has had this six-day rest and says that he is fully recovered. There will be no question as a result of tonight's match."

A capacity crowd was looking forward to the matchup and was treated to an exceptional doubles match after George Lott beat Bruce Barnes in the preliminary, 6–3, 5–5 (the match was ended at that point due to time constraints). Perry and Lott defeated Vines and Barnes, 8–6, 3–6, 6–4.

In the main match of the evening between Vines and Perry (they later entered business together, buying the Beverly Hills Tennis Club), it was apparent that the American had indeed recovered, taking the opening set, 6–3. After shooting out to a 4–1 lead in the second set, Perry came on strong, closing the deficit to 4–3 before eventually winning, 7–5, to tie the match at one set apiece. If the capacity crowd thought Perry now had the advantage, they were mistaken.

Vines, one of the most powerful players of his time with a serve that was clocked at 118 miles per hour—an incredible achievement with the equipment of the day—took a 3–0 lead in the third before winning it, 6–4. He then captured the fourth set easily, winning the final five games in a 6–1 victory that clinched the match, three games to one.

It was his first win of the series after three consecutive losses. Vines, who eventually quit tennis and joined the PGA Tour, becoming one of the better golfers on the circuit, went on to win the American part of the exhibition tour, 32–29, before losing in Europe, 3–6, as the two titans of tennis tied at thirty-five matches each in this historic series.

It was exciting to see the Triangles win their championship in 1976, but these two Hall-of-Fame talents put on quite a show in the Gardens in what was arguably the most exciting night of tennis played in the Steel City.

51

THE BEST PLAY HERE

Duquesne Gardens Hosts Dukes Cagers as Nation's No. 1 Team

By Robert Healy III

Many Western Pennsylvania sports fans were surprised to learn that, when the University of Pittsburgh ascended to the top of the Associated Press men's college basketball rankings on January 5, 2009, it marked the first time a Pittsburgh team had been ranked no. 1 in that poll in roughly fifty-five years. Perhaps even more surprising was the fact that it wasn't Pitt that was the previous no. 1 team.

That would be the crosstown Duquesne Dukes, who, despite taking a back seat to the Panthers in recent decades, were once an elite basketball brand. Duquesne competed annually for national championships in the middle of the twentieth century and sent many players to the professional ranks. The only NCAA Division I basketball team in Western Pennsylvania history (through 2021) to win a national championship tournament are the 1955 Dukes, National Invitation Tournament winners at a time when that tournament's reputation rivaled or even surpassed that of the NCAA's.

The Dukes' run to the top of the AP poll, a rankings system in place since the 1948–49 season, began right after the university reinstated varsity basketball following World War II. After a three-season hiatus due to the war, Duquesne went 20-2 in 1946–47, the best winning percentage among independent teams in major college basketball that season. Duquesne followed that with a 17-6 record the next season and made a case to be ranked by the AP when it stood at 9-1 for the poll's debut on January 18, 1949.

Chuck Cooper (*no. 15 in white, far left*) was one of the first great superstars at Duquesne University. While one of the school's premier players, he made his biggest mark in the NBA, where he not only was the first African American drafted in "1950" but the first to step on a court as an NBA player, which he did on October 18, 1950, in an exhibition game against Baltimore, the first to start an NBA regular-season game and the first to be named to the NBA All-Rookie team. *Courtesy of Duquesne University Athletics.*

The Dukes got enough votes to rank thirtieth in the first AP ranking after defeating unbeaten Akron on January 17. They then played no. 12 Loyola of Chicago on January 24 at home, Duquesne Gardens in Pittsburgh's Oakland area. Duquesne basketball, obviously, had never before faced an opponent ranked by the AP, and it capitalized, topping the Ramblers in overtime, 52–51. Duquesne picked up another win over a highly ranked opponent that season, blowing out unbeaten no. 8 Villanova at the Gardens, 65–37, on January 31. The AP ranked Duquesne as high as no. 17 in 1948–49 and voted it all the way to no. 2 in January 1950 on the team's way to a 16-0 start that season.

The Dukes had a disappointing end to the 1949–50 season, however, finishing 23-6 and appearing in just three AP top-20 rankings the following season. But they got up to no. 3 in February 1952 and finished at no. 9 in the final 1952–53 AP poll.

Duquesne won nine of its last ten games in the 1952–53 season to finish in third place in the NIT, its highest finish in that tournament since 1940. And the Dukes' roster remained loaded for 1953–54.

The 1953–54 Dukes boasted three players with All-America résumés and sparkling futures. Jim Tucker became the first African American (tied with another player) to win an NBA championship and once recorded an NBA triple-double in just seventeen minutes. Dick Ricketts was a no. 1 NBA draft pick in 1955. And Sihugo Green was a no. 1 pick in 1956. Regarding the latter two players, it is the only time (through 2021) that a school has had back-to-back no. 1 NBA selections. Also on the squad was Fletcher Johnson, who had a notable overseas career.

The AP voters identified Duquesne as being a juggernaut and ranked it third and, eventually, second, in December 1953. The Dukes moved to 20-0 after topping Wayne University, 87–56, at the Gardens on February 15, 1954. When the next day's AP and United Press International coaches polls came out, the Dukes were a consensus no. 1.

Duquesne strutted into its next contest, on the road against Geneva College on February 17, as the nation's no. 1 team for the first time in school history. The Dukes cruised, 93–59. Pittsburgh welcomed its conquerors back to Oakland on February 22 for a 79–52 trouncing of Bowling Green behind Tucker's game-high 25 points.

"A season's record crowd of 5,721 packed the Craig Street arena," the *Pittsburgh Post-Gazette* reported of the Bowling Green game, "to see Coach Dudey Moore's Red and Blue machine win its next to last home game and advance to within four box scores of the downtown school's first perfect campaign."

Duquesne failed to achieve a perfect regular season or its ultimate goal, losing the 1954 NIT title game to Holy Cross, 71–62, and finished the season 26-3 and ranked fifth by the AP and third by the coaches.

Despite entering the next season's NIT as the AP's no. 6 and the coaches' no. 7 team, Duquesne finally earned an elusive national title by beating rival Dayton, 70–58, in the championship game.

52

"TV BASKETBALL PARTIES EVERYWHERE"

Live Cameras Capture Dukes Topping Bonnies in Battle of Unbeatens

By Robert Healy III

Radio with pictures, the next logical step after the telegraph without wires.

Inventors and investors spent decades fine-tuning the Televisor and then the television until "TV," as it came to be known, replaced the radio as the standard for in-home entertainment. It was a way to not only hear but also see the actions of athletes and other entertainers from miles away, even in real time.

In the early 1950s, a home without a television set wasn't unheard of. According to TVHistory.tv, only 9 percent of American households had a television in 1950. That number rose to 23.5 percent in 1951, and by 1952, it was at 34.2 percent, or roughly 15.3 million households. That's still quite an audience, and with live radio broadcasts having been a big draw for sports fans for quite some time, there was opportunity for sports on TV to be the next big thing.

The first foray into televised sports came at the Berlin Olympics in 1936, when a limited audience in designated German viewing areas watched action from the Games. In the United States, sports hit TV on May 17, 1939, when the National Broadcasting Company aired moving pictures from the second game of a Columbia-Princeton baseball doubleheader at Columbia's Baker Field to, according to an essay by renowned sportswriter Leonard Koppett on the Columbia website, "the 400 or so sets then capable of receiving its broadcast signal."

Jim Tucker was one of the most celebrated players at Duquesne University in the mid-1950s, but it was in the NBA where he made his most lasting contributions to the game of basketball. In 1955, Tucker became the first African American to play on an NBA championship team, along with Earl Lloyd, when Syracuse captured the crown that season. Tucker also broke the record that year for the quickest triple-double in NBA history, performing the feat in seventeen minutes against the New York Knicks. *Courtesy of Duquesne University Athletics.*

The *New York Times* acknowledged the occasion the next day as "the first regularly-scheduled sporting event to be pictured over the air waves." But the paper reported elsewhere in the same issue, according to Koppett, "that dealers were abandoning attempts to sell television sets to an indifferent public and concentrating their efforts on the rising sale of more elaborate radio sets."

Still, as Koppett writes, the event was "one small step for a broadcasting pioneer, a giant leap for mankind's appetite for spectatoritis," and the prospect of watching live sports in the home spurred more Americans (and American broadcasters) to utilize the new medium.

That included in Pittsburgh, the birthplace of commercial radio (1920) and site of the first live radio broadcasts of baseball (1921) and college football (1921). The Pittsburgh sports scene in the 1950s was mostly drab, with its NFL and MLB teams subpar at best and no NHL or NBA teams. The decade wasn't particularly notable for the University of Pittsburgh's football or men's basketball teams, either, save for a couple of bowl losses by the gridders and a first-round NCAA tournament win by the hoopsters.

So, for many Pittsburgh sports fans, the best show in town was the ultra-competitive Duquesne University men's basketball program, which, by 1950, was nationally ranked and frequently competing in postseason tournaments, even turning down, in 1941 and 1947, NCAA tournament bids but playing in the National Invitation Tournament, considered by many to be the best college basketball event of the era. The *Pittsburgh Press* even called the NIT, in 1952, "basketball's world series."

In 1952, Duquesne was one of the last teams to play in the NIT and NCAA tournament in the same season. (The NCAA banned the practice beginning the next season.) The powerhouse Dukes, ranked fifth in the country in early February 1952, were slated to face no. 4 St. Bonaventure at Pittsburgh's Duquesne Gardens on February 11.

The showdown between the nation's only major undefeated teams was too much for local WDTV to pass up, and it made the Dukes-Bonnies tilt the first televised basketball game to originate from Pittsburgh.

Duquesne won, 69–63, behind a game-high 19 points from Dick Ricketts and 17 and 15 from Jim Tucker and Al Bailey, respectively. The final score was relatively close, but once the Dukes went up, 14–13, in the first half, they held the lead for good, even going up by 12 with 1:30 to play, the *Press* reported.

Though TVs weren't yet in most American households, *Press* sports editor Chester Smith wrote that Pittsburghers found ways to watch—if not in person at the crowded Gardens—with "TV basketball parties everywhere."

In a scene straight out of the twenty-first century, when can't-miss sports are consumed heavily on television either at home or at a bar, Smith wrote on February 12, 1952: "Traffic was unusually light downtown.…Smart burglars confined their operations to the homes of no-TV families. Otherwise they would have been sure to have found somebody at home.

"Video-equipped taprooms and amusement spots did well by themselves. The others didn't."

IT'S MILLER TIME: IN THE PRE-INTERNET AGE, A NEW SEASON MEANT A TRIP TO GUS MILLER'S NEWSSTAND

By Chris Fletcher

Diehard Oakland-ites will talk about the good old days and embrace their inner Rick Sebaks and Tommy Keenes by lamenting places that are gone. Forbes Field was torn down in 1970, making way for the expansion of the University of Pittsburgh. Pitt Stadium met a similar fate, now the site of the Petersen Events Center. A few blocks away, Pirate infielder Frankie Gustine opened an eatery that bore his name and for more than thirty years was the go-to place to meet athletes and celebrities. Also gone is the Syria Mosque, where I saw my fill of '80s acts like X, The Psychedelic Furs and New Order. I was too young to see any of the historic sporting events at the Duquesne Gardens, home to great moments in pre-Penguin hockey and the site of fights by Pittsburgh boxing royalty.

But I still made the trek to Oakland for my sporting fixes, taking the bus across town to welcome each new season by stopping at Gus Miller's Newsstand. For me, that little nondescript building tucked at the corner of Forbes Avenue and Oakland Street was every bit as important as those other icons. It was my source for quarterly bibles from Street & Smith, which would prep me for what to expect in baseball, college football, professional football and professional basketball. It's also where I purchased each sport's *Who's Who* digests and later pored over the stats from the previous season. How else would I know what Mike Easler hit the past four seasons? A trip to Gus Miller's was the equivalent of a sports fan's training camp.

A defensive coordinator for Johnny Majors at the University of Pittsburgh before leaving to run the program at Washington State in 1976, Jackie Sherrill came back to Pitt in 1977, taking over as head coach after Majors left for Tennessee. Sherrill compiled a 50-9-1 mark in five seasons, including three consecutive 11-1 records, before heading off to Texas A&M in 1982. *Courtesy of the University of Pittsburgh Athletics.*

Miller had taken over the space, the former site of a tobacco store, in 1910. At the top of the edifice was a sign that once read "The Just Right." There are also reports that the building served as a brothel at one time (perhaps explaining the "just right" part). Gus Miller's place, though, was a no-nonsense, no-frills newsstand where all generations and all levels of society would stop to pick up a paper, breeze through sports rags or grab some smokes. Yet it was Gus's daughter Myrtle Mae Miller who created a mirthful memento that has since become a hallowed collector's item. She was the woman behind the Green Weenie. Those green, plastic, hot-dog-shaped rattles supposedly held mystical powers when fans shook them to jinx Pirate opponents at Forbes Field. Every true Buc fan had one during the 1960 world championship season. Perhaps Ralph Terry was "rattled" when he served up Bill Mazeroski's series-clinching blast. Still, it's safe to say that the Green Weenie begat the Terrible Towel, as Myron Cope borrowed some magic from Myrtle Mae.

I was looking for similar magic, picking up the 1980 *Street & Smith Pro Football Guide* with Steeler quarterback Terry Bradshaw on the cover. I was excited for a three-peat, as were the editors. However, we all missed the fact that the Steelers had struggled to beat a good but not great Los Angeles Rams team in the Super Bowl a few months earlier. In 1980, the Steelers underachieved, or maybe age just caught up with them. For the first time in nearly a decade, they missed the playoffs, and they ushered in an era of mediocrity.

Two years later, another Pittsburgh quarterback graced the cover of the *Street & Smith College Football Guide*, this time Pitt's Dan Marino. I snapped it up, eagerly awaiting another championship that would not be. Apparently, before the *Sports Illustrated* and Madden jinxes, there was the *Street & Smith* jinx. Pitt came into the season ranked no. 1, but after starting 7-0, the Panthers lost at home to an unranked Notre Dame team, 31–16. It closed the season with disappointing losses at no. 2 Penn State (19-10) and in the Cotton Bowl against no. 4 SMU.

The funny thing is, despite all the stats, stories and predictions available in today's information age, I still think back to trips to Gus Miller's. I also remember it as the newsstand where I bought the first issue of *Pittsburgh* magazine that I edited. It's the tactile experience of flipping through a magazine that stays with you and that you miss. You'll never have such an emotional connection to a Google search.

FIRST OR NOT: GREENLEE FIELD
HOUSED CHAMPIONS

By David Finoli

Greenlee Field, home of the Pittsburgh Crawfords, was not in Oakland, so it didn't qualify for inclusion in the main part of this book. But since it was only a mile outside of Oakland in the Hill District between Bedford Avenue and Chauncey Street, and because it housed champions and was an important part of the city's sports history, it deserves the opportunity for its tale to be told.

It is said that Greenlee Field was the first Black-built and Black-owned stadium in the country. Historian and author Bill Ranier explained in his chapter "Because the Marker Says So" in our book *Pittsburgh Sports Firsts* that there may have been a couple stadiums that came first. He found that there was a stadium in Cleveland named Tate Field, home of the Cleveland Tate Stars, that was built by an African American and owned by George Tate. He also found that a park built by the man who constructed Greenlee Field, Louis Bellinger, built one for the Pittsburgh Keystones a year before Tate Field. Whether or not these two stadiums were actually of major league quality has always been the question. But we do know that Greenlee Field was.

They began to build it in 1931, and Greenlee was officially opened on April 29, 1932, when the New York Black Yankees beat the Crawfords, 1–0. Gus Greenlee, the man for whom the facility is named, decided to build the stadium in the Hill District for two reasons. He was playing at Ammon

Sitting in front of his Pittsburgh Pirates at spring training is general manager Branch Rickey. While known for setting up a minor league system, which he was the first to do in St. Louis, and the historic signing of Jackie Robinson with the Brooklyn Dodgers, Rickey played a major part in forming the 1960 World Series champion Pittsburgh Pirates. *Courtesy of the Pittsburgh Pirates.*

Field for most of his contests and leased Forbes Field for the bigger contests. Among the problems this arrangement presented was that Ammon was not a big enough facility for the marquee contests. And Forbes Field was expensive and didn't allow Black players to use the clubhouse. It was also in Oakland, which was too far from the neighborhoods that housed the fans of the team, and this kept most of them away. Greenlee decided to build a new stadium in the Hill District to solve most of these issues.

The stadium housed 6,500 fans and had the following dimensions: 338 feet to right field, 410 to center and 342 feet to the left-field wall. It was built of concrete and steel, but as Ranier stated in his chapter, it had a "back wall partially made of tin." Another interesting feature of the facility was a 1-foot right-field wall where the bleachers sat right up against it.

Housing also the Homestead Grays at times as well as the Pittsburgh Steelers (at the time called the Pirates), who used it for in-season practices, the venue's main tenant was the Pittsburgh Crawfords, who fielded arguably the best teams in Negro League history between 1934 and 1936.

Unfortunately, many of Greenlee's best players left for much higher salaries in the Dominican Republic in 1937. Then other financial issues led to the Crawfords being moved to Toledo. A year later, in 1938, Greenlee Field was razed to make room for a low-cost housing development called Bedford Dwellings.

Six years is a short life for an athletic facility. As stated, it wasn't located in Oakland. But there was quite a bit of championship baseball played there during this period. Today, all that remains is a historical marker claiming it to be the first African American–owned stadium in Negro League history. Even though others say that may not be true, it was the home of champions. That is something no one can dispute.

BIBLIOGRAPHY

Newspapers

Pittsburgh Post-Gazette
Pittsburgh Press
Tribune Review (Pittsburgh, PA)

Magazines

NCAA Football Guide
The Sporting News
Sports Illustrated

Websites

American Hockey League. www.theahl.com.
The Athletic. www.theathletic.com.
Baseball Reference. www.baseball-reference.com.
Basketball Reference. www.basketball-reference.com.
Bleacher Report. www.bleacherreport.com.
Duquesne University Athletics. www.goduquesne.com.
ESPN. www.espn.com.
HockeyDB.com. www.hockeydb.com.
Hockey Reference. www.hockey-reference.com.
Major League Baseball. www.mlb.com.
National Football League. www.nfl.com.

National Hockey League. www.nhl.com.
Pittsburgh Hockey. www.pittsburghhockey.net.
Pittsburgh Penguins. www.pittsburghpenguins.com.
Pittsburgh Pirates. www.pittsburghpirates.com.
Pittsburgh Steelers. www.pittsburghsteelers.com.
The Ringer. www.theringer.com.
Society for American Baseball Research. www.sabr.org.
Trib Live. www.triblive.com.
Undefeated. www.undefeated.com.
University of Pittsburgh Athletics. www.pittsburghpanthers.com.

Media Guides

Duquesne University Basketball
Pittsburgh Penguins
Pittsburgh Pirates
Pittsburgh Steelers
University of Pittsburgh Basketball
University of Pittsburgh Football

Books

Finoli, David. *Classic Pens*. Kent, OH: Kent State University Press, 2017.
———. *Pittsburgh's Greatest Athletes*. Charleston, SC: The History Press, 2018.
———. *Pittsburgh's Greatest Teams*. Charleston, SC: The History Press, 2017.
———. *When Pitt Ruled the Gridiron*. Jefferson, NC: McFarland & Company, 2014.
Finoli, David, and Bill Ranier. *The Pittsburgh Pirates Encyclopedia*. N.p.: Sports Publishing Inc., 2015.
Finoli, David, and Chris Fletcher. *Steel City Gridirons*. Pittsburgh, PA: Towers Maguire Publishing, 2006.
Finoli, David, and Chuck Cooper III. *Breaking Barriers: The Chuck Cooper Story*. Seattle, WA: Amazon Publishing, 2020.
Finoli, David, and Robert Healy III. *Kings on the Bluff*. Seattle, WA: Createspace Press, 2017.

ABOUT THE AUTHORS

Having grown up in Greensburg, Pennsylvania, **DAVID FINOLI** is a passionate fan of Western Pennsylvania sports, which has been the subject of most of the books he has produced. A graduate of the Duquesne University School of Journalism, where he is featured on the "Wall of Fame" in Duquesne's journalism and multimedia department, Finoli has penned thirty-five books that have highlighted the stories of the great franchises in this area, such as the Pirates, Penguins, Steelers, Duquesne basketball and Pitt football, to name a few. In one of his latest books, *Pittsburgh's Greatest Players*, he not only ranks the top fifty players in Western Pennsylvania history but also includes a list of every Hall-of-Fame athlete who represented the area. Winner of *Pittsburgh Magazine*'s Best of the 'Burgh local author award for 2018, Finoli lives in Monroeville, Pennsylvania, with his wife, Vivian. He also has three children, Tony, Cara, Matt; his daughter in-law Chynna; and three grandchildren, River, Emmy and Ellie.

TOM ROONEY had three stretches of duty at the Civic Arena. As an usher while matriculating across the way at Duquesne University, he worked at least one hundred events a year for four years (1969–73), a great way to see his beloved Penguins and actually get paid for it. For a decade (1981–90), he worked for the DeBartolo-owned Civic Arena Corporation, running and promoting events and marketing teams like the Pens, soccer Spirit and indoor football Gladiators. He spent four more years (1999–2003) working for Mario Lemieux as president of the Pens. Under the dome was his home away from home.

CHRIS FLETCHER, based in Forest Hills, Pennsylvania, is a writer, marketer, fundraiser and all-around swell guy. He is the former publisher and editor of *Pittsburgh Magazine*, where Chris won ten Golden Quill Awards. Under his direction, the magazine earned the prestigious White Award as the country's top city magazine in 1995 from the City and Regional Magazine Association. Fletcher also teamed up with David Finoli to author two other sports books, *Steel City Gridirons* and *The Steel City 500*. A 1984 graduate of Duquesne University's journalism program, Chris still dreams of catching one more contest in the old Civic Arena (provided it wouldn't be in one of the obstructed-view seats).

ROBERT EDWARD HEALY III, a Pittsburgh native, is a professor in the Media department at Duquesne University, where he heads Duquesne's Sports Information and Media program. Prior to teaching, Robert worked as a sports information director and as a news reporter. He and his daughters, Rhiannon and Josephine, live in Pittsburgh's South Hills area.

DOUGLAS CAVANAUGH is a freelance writer living in Los Angeles. His most recent projects include collaborating on the book *Rooney-McGinley Boxing Club* with Art Rooney Jr., as well as his own book, *Pittsburgh Boxing: A Pictorial History*. He currently runs a popular Pittsburgh boxing history page on Facebook.